EDITED BY
BLAINE BROWNELL

Transmaterial

A CATALOG
OF MATERIALS
THAT
REDEFINE
OUR
PHYSICAL
ENVIRONMENT

PRINCETON ARCHITECTURAL PRESS
NEW YORK

TO HEATHER, BLAINE, & DAVIS

Published by
Princeton Architectural Press
37 East Seventh Street, New York, NY 10003

For a free catalog of books, call 1-800-722-6657
Visit our web site at www.papress.com

Editing: Jennifer N. Thompson
Editorial Assistance: Dorothy Ball, Becca Casbon
Design: Paul G. Wagner

Special thanks to: Nettie Aljian, Dorothy Ball,
Nicola Bednarek, Janet Behning, Megan Carey, Becca Casbon,
Penny (Yuen Pik) Chu, Russell Fernandez, Jan Haux,
Clare Jacobson, John King, Mark Lamster, Nancy Eklund Later,
Linda Lee, Katharine Myers, Lauren Nelson, Jane Sheinman,
Scott Tennent, Joe Weston, and Deb Wood of
Princeton Architectural Press —Kevin C. Lippert, publisher

Library of Congress Cataloging-in-Publication Data

Brownell, Blaine Erickson, 1970–
Transmaterial : a catalog of materials that redefine
our physical environment / Blaine E. Brownell.
p. cm.
Includes index.
ISBN 1-56898-563-0
1. Materials—Technological innovations.
2. Materials—Catalogs.
I. Title.
TA403.6.B76 2006
620.1′1—dc22

2005025497

TABLE OF CONTENTS

INTRODUCTION: A MATERIAL REVOLUTION

You may have noticed it when passing by an electroluminescent store display, hearing about your neighbor's recycled-glass countertops, using your new conductive plastic-powered mobile phone, or reading about self-cleaning paint: we live in a time of unprecedented material innovations that are affecting our lives. The accelerated pace of these innovations and the breadth of their applications have enhanced our awareness about new products and the ways in which they are transforming our physical environment. In fact, there are so many new and unusual materials in the marketplace that a cottage industry of boutique services has emerged to assess and endorse them. While it is difficult to project real numbers, it has become a widely held belief that more new products have been developed in the last twenty years than in the prior history of materials science.

Indeed, when one evaluates the diverse and fantastic range of materials available today, one realizes the extent of humanity's unwavering pursuit of innovation. Rather than a fixed catalog of products, one sees a constantly shifting array of materials, which offer continual improvements upon known standards or render those standards obsolete. Innovation itself assumes a wide variety of forms; for example, a scientist may stumble upon a new product chemistry while attempting to solve an unrelated problem; an architect may develop a new process to satisfy a need for which there is no current solution; or a manufacturer may augment a product's performance based on a discovery within another field. Whatever the method, one could make a case that there is a veritable material revolution underway, and this revolution is affecting all industries. No traditional product or building system is safe from scrutiny, as all materials are being closely studied for enhancement or replacement.

MOTIVATIONS

How did this groundswell of innovation develop? One simple view is that while materials science has existed since the stone age, it is simply advancing at an accelerated pace like other technologies, and this pace has finally become conspicuous. In this sense, material innovation may be said to parallel Moore's Law, which states that computational power follows an accelerated curve. (After all, advances in digital technology have also spawned a multitude of new methodologies for creating and modifying products.)

Another view considers "the NASA effect," in which significant innovations developed for aerospace or military applications are repurposed for consumer uses. Markets which support these new applications often take decades to mature, and some Apollo-era technologies are just now becoming commercially viable in the public sector. Memory Foam, for example, was originally developed for astronauts to delay the physical fatigue experienced during space flight, but it is now a popular material for mattresses and sporting equipment.

One of the most interesting explanations for this wave of material awareness is a growing consciousness about the world's natural limits. Industrial-era technology considered raw resources to be cheap and endlessly renewable, with little thought given to the ill-effects generated by the by-products of industrial processes. In our current postindustrial age, however, we understand the interdependency of global systems and have become keenly aware of the earth's dwindling raw materials, diminishing fossil fuels, and the problems associated with industrial waste. Many new product innovations, therefore, are based on using less raw material and energy, repurposing existing materials into new forms, and creating materials which are less toxic for the environment. A related trend is the study of biomimicry, in which science looks to natural processes for inspiration, especially at the cellular or biochemical level.

Yet another motive for invention is inherently phenomenological. Many new products are created out of the desire to achieve a particular aesthetic or psychological effect, without a particular pragmatic need in mind. This motivation explains the proliferation of translucent composite materials, for example, which are often used to impart a luminous, enigmatic quality to their surroundings. This convention-defying development also represents a growing desire to bring art into life.

TRENDS

Within the ever-changing inventory of new products, several broad classifications arise that elucidate the material transformations that are occurring. These classifications are interesting because they highlight important themes, which might be shared between dissimilar products. For example, an aluminum floor system and polypropylene chair are comprised of different substances, but they could be similarly important in their use of recycled materials. The seven broad categories I have proposed are as follows:

1) ULTRAPERFORMING

Throughout human history, material innovation has been defined by the persistent testing of limits. Ultraperforming materials are those which are stronger, lighter, more durable, and more flexible than their conventional counterparts. These materials are important because they shatter known boundaries and necessitate new thinking about the shaping of our physical environment.

Interestingly enough, one of the most significant trends in material innovation is actually dematerialization. The ongoing pursuit of thinner, more porous, and less opaque products indicates a notable movement toward greater exposure and ephemerality.

It should come as no surprise that ultraperforming materials are generally expensive and difficult to obtain, although many of these products are being developed for a broad market.

2) MULTIDIMENSIONAL

Obviously materials are physically defined by three dimensions, but many products have long been conceived as a collection of flat planes that define space and function.

A new trend highlights the exploitation of the z-axis in the manufacturing of a wide variety of materials, ranging from fabrics to wall and ceiling treatments. One reason for this development is that greater depth allows thin materials to become more structurally stable. In addition, materials with enhanced texture and richness are more visually interesting.

Augmented dimensionality will likely be a growing movement, especially considering the technological trends toward miniaturization, systems integration, and prefabrication.

3) REPURPOSED

Repurposed materials may be defined as surrogates, or materials that are used in the place of others conventionally used in an application.

Repurposed materials provide several benefits, such as replacing precious raw materials with less precious, more plentiful ones; diverting products from the waste stream; implementing less toxic manufacturing processes; and simply defying convention. A subset of this group is considered repurposed in terms of its functionality, such as tables that become light sources and art that becomes furniture.

As a trend, repurposing is important because it underscores the desire for adaptability, as well as an increasing awareness of our limited resources. While the performance of repurposed materials is not always identical to that of the products they replace, sometimes new and unexpected benefits arise from their use.

4) RECOMBINANT

Recombinant materials consist of two or more different materials that act in harmony to create a product that performs greater than the sum of its parts. Such hybrids are created when inexpensive or recyclable products are used as "filler"; when a combination allows for the achievement of multiple functions; when a precious resource may be emulated by combining less precious materials; or when different materials act in symbiosis to exhibit high-performance characteristics.

Recombinant materials have long proven their performance in the construction industry. Reinforced concrete, which benefits from the compressive strength and fireproof qualities of concrete and the tensile strength of steel, is a classic recombination. The success of recombinant materials is based on their reliable integration, which is not always predictable. Moreover, they are often comprised of down-cycled components which may be difficult, if not impossible, to re-extract. However, the continued value exhibited by many such hybrids is evidence of a growing trend.

5) INTELLIGENT

Intelligent is a catch-all term for materials that are designed to improve their environment and that often take inspiration from biological systems. They can act actively or passively, and they can be high-tech or low-tech. Many materials in this category indicate a growing focus on manipulation at the microscopic scale.

Intelligence is not used here to describe products that have autonomous computational power, but rather products which are inherently smart by design. The varied list of benefits provided by materials featured here includes pollution reduction, water purification, solar radiation control, natural ventilation, and power generation. An intelligent product may simply be a flexible or modular system that adds value throughout its life cycle.

Intelligent materials are significant because their designers and manufacturers are acknowledging the importance of increased social and environmental stewardship, not to mention the desire to improve upon old models.

6) TRANSFORMATIONAL

Transformational materials undergo a physical metamorphosis based on environmental stimuli. This change may occur automatically based on the properties of the material, or it may be user-driven.

Like intelligent materials, transformational materials provide a variety of benefits, including waste reduction, enhanced ergonomics, solar control, and illumination, as well as interesting phenomenological effects. Transformational products are important because they offer multiple functions where one would be expected, they provide benefits that few might have imagined, and they simply make us view the world differently.

7) INTERFACIAL

The interface has been a popular design focus since the birth of the digital age. As we spend increased amounts of time interacting with computer-based tools and environments, the bridges that facilitate the interaction between physical and virtual worlds are subject to increased scrutiny. Interfacial materials, products, and systems navigate this bridge between the two realms.

So-called interfacial products may be virtual instruments that control material manufacturing, or physical manifestations of digital fabrications. These tools are significant because they provide unprecedented capabilities, such as enhancing technology-infused work environments, rapid-prototyping complex shapes, integrating digital imagery within physical objects, and making the invisible visible.

Interfacial materials are also relevant because they employ the latest computing and communications technologies and therefore are indicative of society's future trajectory. Like the hardware and software glitches we know too well, interfacial materials are not infallible, but they expand our capabilities into uncharted territory.

BACKGROUND

Unlike the artist, who interacts directly with his or her palette, the architect is one step removed from the physical substance that makes architecture. This synapse often breeds ignorance about what materials are available or what properties they possess, which is reinforced by the fact that most buildings are still comprised of relatively conventional products and systems despite the wide variety available. Compounding this problem is the fact that architectural education has generally failed to provide students with a sufficient knowledge of materials, especially within U.S.–based institutions.

The Transmaterial project originated from humble beginnings, for I realized the importance of studying materials when faced with my own ignorance about them. After completing my graduate studies, I had the privilege of working with Mark Wamble, who now leads the firm Interloop Design with Dawn Finley in Houston. When I collaborated with Mark on the design for a prominent project, Mark put me in charge of materials research. He told me to "be a detective," and to grill product representatives with tough, thoughtful questions. Unfortunately, I felt ill-prepared for the job at the time.

However, it didn't take long for me to realize that conventional thinking about materials in architectural practice is severely limited. It intrigued me that countless innovative products are being developed, yet relatively few are utilized in building construction. I now say that if architecture is indeed the mother of the arts, then it is also the great-grandchild of the sciences. The rampant conservatism throughout the construction industry has been stifling for architects, and therefore many of us know less than we should about innovative materials.

My experience working with Mark was fantastic, however, because he knew the value that material innovation has for design, and he persuaded the design team, client, and contractor to develop a new level of appreciation for this kind of materials research. It was this positive experience that inspired me to develop a catalog of innovative products that could serve as a fundamental palette for future projects.

About five years ago, I forced myself into the habit of investigating new items every week, which I learned to find via web sites, print publications, and colleague referrals. When I began to share these discoveries in the form of a weekly email newsletter, I encouraged my friends to share their discoveries as well. Now, I feel fortunate to be part of a broad global network of fascinating individuals who share an interest in material innovation.

It is unfortunate that, like many fields, the profession of architecture is plagued by the selfish hoarding of knowledge. However, I believe that the more we all share, the greater our chances are of improving the standards for architecture and design in general.

Transmaterial was designed to be accessible, engaging, inspiring, thought-provoking, and informative. My colleagues requested that it be like a portable travel guide rather than comprehensive or exhaustive in nature (which it could never be); this book is most effective if it is used to spark new ideas or illuminate current trends. Most importantly, this book is conceived as a brief snapshot within an ongoing effort to learn about and celebrate innovative materials, which is reflected on my web site at www.transstudio.com as well as the companion program developed by Princeton Architectural Press at www.materialsmonthly.com.

The recent interest in new materials has the potential to dislodge the conservative mindset we face today. Thanks to the sustainability movement, as well as the various cottage industries that have surfaced for the sake of providing material knowledge, clients, consultants, and building departments are already adopting more progressive views about what is possible in their projects. Therefore, I believe it is paramount that we inform ourselves about innovative materials and methods so that extraordinary buildings and products can become the norm within our physical environment, rather than the exception.

Blaine E. Brownell

PRODUCT PAGE KEY

A

FOAM

N° 066000-007

B

D Plastic

3D VOLUMETRIC POLYURETHANE ELEMENT FOR INTERIORS

C

E OMA developed Foam as part of their work for Prada. In addition to the design of new spatial typologies, the development of new materials expands the interior palette of the new Prada epicenter stores. Ranging from translucent cast resin for shelves to bubble-textured silicone floor mats, the creation of this new substance manifests a radical redefinition of surface and material.

Foam is a polyurethane cast of an aggregate condition between solid and void. It is both a regular and irregular structure of spongelike consistency that can be cast in stages from hard to soft, and from transparent to opaque. It forms a substance that can be used to build objects as well as entire spaces, a further interpretation of solid and void.

Foam was developed beginning with an architectural model using a regular cleaning sponge. Because the visual effect of this backlit texture was very intriguing, OMA initiated an extensive search to recreate this material in 1:1 scale. The architect made hundreds of prototypes in order to test hole sizes, percentages of openness, translucencies, depths, colors, etc.

In its multiple and varied manifestations, Foam offers a new definition of functional and visual properties between artificial and natural, irregular and regular, transparent and opaque, translucent and solid, flexible and rigid qualities in the design of interior environments.

G INTELLIGENT MATERIAL

F

H CONTENTS
100% polyurethane

APPLICATIONS
Interior finish, furniture, light object

TYPES / SIZES
4'–6" × 9' × 4"
(1.4 m × 2.7 m × 10 cm)

LIMITATIONS
Developed exclusively for Prada

CONTACT
Office for Metropolitan Architecture
Heer Bokelweg 149
Rotterdam, 3032 AD
The Netherlands
Tel: +31-10-243 8200
www.oma.nl
office@oma.nl

A. NAME

The trademarked name of the particular entry being featured

B. NUMBER (N°)

This nine-digit identification number is unique to each entry. The first six digits are based on the new *MasterFormat* material classification system, published June 8, 2004, by the Construction Specifications Institute. The last three digits are used to identify each product within a serial list. This numbering system is congruent with the Materials Monthly program, also published by Princeton Architectural Press.

C. DESCRIPTION

A brief, generic explanation of each entry

D. CATEGORY

Refers to the basic materiality of the product, such as concrete, metal, or plastic; it is the primary means of organization in this book.

E. SUMMARY

A basic text description of each entry

F. TREND

This field assigns one of the seven trends mentioned in the introduction to each entry: ultraperforming, multidimensional, repurposed, recombinant, intelligent, transformational, or interfacial.

G. TYPE

Defines each entry as a material, product, or process

H. ADDITIONAL DATA

The following information is also used to describe product entries: contents, applications, types or sizes, environmental benefits, industry tests or examinations, limitations, and manufacturer contact information.

01: **CONCRETE**

LOW-IMPACT FOUNDATION TECHNOLOGY

The Pin Foundation Diamond Pier is a precast concrete pier and steel pin system that provides a solid foundation that reaches deep into the ground without digging. The pier components are light enough to hand-carry to the site, and the installation is simple, requiring only hand tools and a few minutes of time.

The development of Pin Foundation's unique technology began more than two decades ago in an effort to design foundation systems that would eliminate excavation and minimize the disruption of the existing soil's state and natural topography. These soils have developed over many centuries and provide critical natural storage and filtering for rainfall. Digging alters these soil characteristics, and Diamond Piers offer a cost-effective solution for installing a reliable and durable foundation without degrading streams and water quality.

The piers can be installed in any native soil or compacted fill—even in frost, expansive, or saturated soils often deemed too marginal for traditional construction. Predetermined pin lengths are driven through slots in the pier that has been installed at grade. There are two pier sizes: The DP-50 and DP-100, weighing fifty and one hundred pounds, respectively. The DP-50 can achieve a maximum capacity of four thousand pounds, while the DP-100 can achieve a maximum capacity of eight thousand pounds. The soils encountered and the length of the pin installed will determine the pier's capacity.

CONTENTS
Concrete, steel, PVC

APPLICATIONS
Building foundations

TYPES / SIZES
DP-50: 10.5" (27 cm) square at midpoint, 11" (28 cm) high, 50 lbs (23 kg), pin length varies;
DP-100: 13" (33 cm) square at midpoint, 14" (35.5 cm) high, 100 lbs (45 kg), pin length varies

ENVIRONMENTAL
Minimal impact on existing soils

CONTACT
Pin Foundations, Inc.
8607 58th Avenue NW
Gig Harbor, WA 98332
Tel: 253-858-8809
www.pinfoundations.com
pinfound@pinfoundations.com

ULTRA HIGH-PERFORMANCE CONCRETE

ULTRAPERFORMING MATERIAL

Ductal is a new material technology that offers ductility, strength, and durability while providing moldable products with a quality surface. Compressive strengths reach up to 30,000 psi (200 MPa) and flexural strengths reach up to 7,000 psi (50 MPa). With Ductal, it is possible to create thinner sections, longer spans, and higher structures, which are lighter, more graceful and innovative in geometry, and have superior durability and impermeability against corrosion, abrasion, and impact.

Ductal provides precasters with opportunities to improve many existing products and to manufacture new lines of products that will compete with stainless steel, cast iron, ceramics, and others. By utilizing its superior properties, Ductal solutions can eliminate passive reinforcing steel and experience reduced global construction costs, formwork, labor, and maintenance, resulting in benefits such as improved construction safety, speed of construction, and extended life.

CONTENTS

Cement, silica fume, sand, superplasticizer, water, ground quartz, mineral fibers, and other fibers

APPLICATIONS

Architectural wall panels, acoustic panels, thin-shelled canopy systems, footbridges, columns, sculptures, site furniture, anchor plates

ENVIRONMENTAL

Partially manufactured from recycled industrial by-products with up to 75% reduction in CO_2 emissions compared to conventional solutions

LIMITATIONS

Not for cast-in-place or spray applications

CONTACT

Lafarge
North America Inc.
12950 Worldgate Drive
Suite 500
Herndon, VA 20170
Tel: 866-238-2825
www.imagineductal.com
ductal@lafarge-na.com

ECO-CEMENT

CARBON DIOXIDE–ABSORBING CEMENT

Developed by John Harrison of TecEco, Eco-Cement is made by blending reactive magnesium oxide with conventional hydraulic cements. Mimicking nature, Eco-Cement concretes absorb large amounts of carbon dioxide from the atmosphere in order to harden into materials used for the built environment. As Eco-Cements are also chemically benign, large amounts of various wastes can be incorporated into the concrete matrix. The Eco-Cement technology offers partial solutions for global warming, climate change, waste, and cost-effective mass housing.

CONTENTS

High magnesium-oxide cement

APPLICATIONS

Cast-in-place concrete, precast concrete, concrete masonry

TYPES / SIZES

Eco-Cement, Eco-Masonry, Enviro-Cement, Tec-Cement

ENVIRONMENTAL

Absorbs greenhouse gas, incorporates industrial waste

CONTACT

TecEco Pty. Ltd.
497 Main Road
Glenorchy, TAS 7010
Australia
Tel: +61 3 62497868
www.tececo.com

ECOSMART

HIGH-VOLUME FLY-ASH CONCRETE

Concrete, a universal construction material synonymous with strength and longevity, is relatively benign in nature. However, the production of Portland cement, which is an essential constituent of concrete, leads to the release of significant amounts of carbon dioxide into the atmosphere (producing one ton of Portland cement produces about one ton of carbon dioxide).

Worldwide, cement manufacturing accounts for approximately eight percent of global carbon dioxide annual emissions. The use of concrete is expected to grow in the foreseeable future, but this growth needs to be compatible with environmental protection and sustainability.

It is widely accepted that using reclaimed industrial by-products such as fly ash, silica fume, and slag, commonly called supplementary cementing materials (SCM), can reduce the amount of cement needed to make concrete, and hence reduce its carbon dioxide signature. Using SCMs in concrete not only has the potential to reduce greenhouse gas emissions, but also to improve long-term strength and durability characteristics, and it may result in a more economical concrete than conventional Portland-cement concrete. Moreover, industrial by-products are redirected from the wastestream.

CONTENTS

Up to 80% of cement can be replaced with supplementary cementing materials (SCM), such as fly ash, silica fume, and slag

APPLICATIONS

Best for mass elements and applications where low permeability is required for durability

ENVIRONMENTAL

Reduces greenhouse gas emissions, improves the long-term strength and durability characteristics of concrete, and reduces the need for landfilling what would otherwise be waste materials.

TESTS / EXAMINATIONS

CSA A23.1-04

LIMITATIONS

The strength development of concrete incorporating high volumes of SCMs may be slower than that of conventional concrete, and this retarding effect will be increased on cooler days.

CONTACT

Ecosmart Foundation Inc.
501-402 West Pender Street
Vancouver, BC V6B 1T6
Canada
Tel: 604-689-4021
www.ecosmart.ca
information@ecosmart.ca

RECYCLED INSULATING CONCRETE FORMS

Faswall forms are used for building insulated reinforced concrete structures for both residential and commercial construction.

The recycled wood chip–based cement form provides a four-hour fire rating. The forms contribute zero percent to flame spread, smoke development, and fuel contribution. Because the forms are designed to breathe, they prevent condensation build-up and mold growth. They are also termite proof.

Faswall forms may be constructed using conventional carpenter tools. Stucco and plaster may be applied without lathing, and siding and drywall may be nailed directly to the Faswall surface. Faswall forms also provide significant tornado, hurricane, and earthquake resistance.

CONTENTS
85% recycled waste wood chips, 15% Portland cement

APPLICATIONS
Cast-in-place concrete construction

TYPES / SIZES
16 × 11 × 8" (41 × 28 × 20 cm), 16 × 8 × 8" (41 × 20 × 20 cm), 20 × 8 × 8" (51 × 20 × 20 cm)
Superinsulating WF: 24 × 12 × 12" (61 × 30.5 × 30.5 cm)

ENVIRONMENTAL
Utilizes recycled post-consumer waste wood chips from shipping pallets, saw mill waste and/or forest clearings processed with an all-natural, non-toxic clay emulsion

TESTS / EXAMINATIONS
ASTM E 84-89, E 119-88, C423-90, E 795-91, and C 666

CONTACT
K-X Faswall International Corporation
PO Box 328
Montmorenci, SC 29839
Tel: 803-642-8142
www.faswall.com
faswall@faswall.com

FEATHERPANEL

LIGHTWEIGHT ARCHITECTURAL STONE

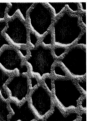

Due to more stringent governmental regulations, the exhaustion of natural resources, and enhanced economic objectives, stone is being replaced by alternative materials in architecture and design. Stonelab has developed a lightweight architectural stone called Featherpanel, which is cast in high-precision molds. The use of 3D laser-cut patterns or embossed steel panels allow for a wide variety of textures, shapes, patterns, colors, and sizes.

Featherpanel is less expensive and eighty-five percent lighter than natural stone. It also may be attached via adhesive rather than traditional anchoring systems and may be modified with regular woodworking tools. Moreover, its light weight makes the product particularly appealing from a transportation and construction standpoint.

CONTENTS

75% constructive foam and reinforcement layers, 25% lightweight poly-cementitious mortar

APPLICATIONS

Decorative finishing, thermal and acoustic insulation, walls, floors, ceilings, cladding, paving, roofing

ENVIRONMENTAL

100% recyclable, energy-saving, conserves natural sources

CONTACT

Stonelab
PO Box 3724
Amsterdam, 1001 AM
The Netherlands
Tel: +0031 20 6382226
www.stonelab.nl
marketing@stonelab.nl

INTAGLIO COMPOSITES

PHOTOGRAPHIC IMAGING IN CONCRETE

Employing a combination of chemistry, high-tech equipment, concrete expertise, and graphical technology, Intaglio Composites can permanently integrate any high-resolution image into the surface of precast concrete. The exposed aggregate of the concrete surface effectively becomes the transferred image; therefore, the aggregate size is determined based on the amount of desired image detail and surface image depth.

Intaglio Composites uses a high-performance self-consolidating concrete (SCC) to create a higher-strength, denser, less-permeable concrete. They also use an unlimited range of pigments and additional pozzolanic materials to produce a high-quality finish in order to achieve the greatest contrast between the smooth surface and the etched impressions in the concrete. The imagery selected is the most important aspect of this process since contrast, clarity, and quality dictate the outcome of any work.

CONTENTS
Concrete

APPLICATIONS
Vertical or horizontal applications

TYPES / SIZES
Currently only flat surfaces; developing a 360° application for columns and ceilings

ENVIRONMENTAL
Recycled matrix

CONTACT
Intaglio Composites
3101 Pleasant Valley Lane
Suite B
Arlington, TX 76015
Tel: 817-784-8878
www.intaglio
composites.com

LODESTONE

PRECAST MASONRY UNITS

Dan Fette developed LodeStone in order to achieve the appearance of natural stone while providing the consistency and economy of a modular, environmentally sensitive building product. LodeStone's environmental benefit arises primarily from the composition of its blended cement, which uses Class C fly ash material as the principal binder.

LodeStone's "Chiseled Face" veneer blocks project outward irregularly and create deep shadows, which change as the light shifts throughout the day. "Smooth Face" blocks provide a taut, crisp finish similar to honed-faced concrete blocks.

CONTENTS
Sand, blended cement, limestone crusher fines

APPLICATIONS
Exterior and interior masonry veneer installations

TYPES / SIZES
"Chiseled Face" and "Smooth Face" veneer blocks ranging in size from nominal 12 × 8" (30.5 × 20 cm) to 32 × 16" (81 × 41 cm)

ENVIRONMENTAL
80% of blended cement comprised of industrial recycled material (non-toxic)

TESTS / EXAMINATIONS
ASTM C67, C1194, C1195

LIMITATIONS
Not recommended for use below grade

CONTACT
LodeStone Companies
2708 Glenwood Lane
Denton, TX 76209
Tel: 940-483-1761
www.lodestoneproducts.com

PIXEL PANELS

TRANSLUCENT CONCRETE

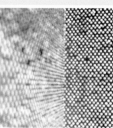

Developed by Bill Price, Pixel Panels are one manifestation of the broader family of products called Translucent Concrete and Transparent Concrete, all of which seek to make concrete a light-transmissive medium. Pixel Panels use concrete as a binder within which a uniform array of polymers is added to provide translucency at a given viewing distance. The ratio of concrete to polymer may be varied to allow for limitless variations (ratios as high as twenty-five percent polymer have been achieved).

CONTENTS
92.5% concrete, 7.5% polymer

APPLICATIONS
Various building applications: walls, floors, ceilings, etc.

TYPES / SIZES
4 × 4 × 1/4" (10 × 10 × .6 cm) minimum panel size; 8' × 10' × 8" (2.4 m × 3 m × 20 cm) maximum panel size

ENVIRONMENTAL
Natural daylighting applications, reduction of energy costs

LIMITATIONS
Exterior applications still being tested

CONTACT
BPZ
12110 Queensbury Lane
Houston, TX 77024
Tel: 713-823-9582
www.translucent
concrete.com

INSULATED CONCRETE FORM

Rastra panels are large building blocks with a grid of internal channels that serve as a stay-in-place wall form for residential and commercial structures. Once a complete floor is set in place, the channels are reinforced and concrete is poured to achieve any desired strength. A Rastra wall is capable of withstanding earthquakes, hurricanes, and other forces of nature because the system of channels is designed to provide maximum strength with a minimum amount of concrete.

The Rastra panels are made of recycled post-consumer foam plastics placed in a cement matrix. This composition unifies the best properties for a wall; it is durable, lightweight, and quick to install and also provides high thermal and acoustic insulation. Rastra is resistant to fire, mold, insects, and rodents. It also has a cementitious surface to which stucco adheres well.

CONTENTS
Recycled foam plastic (85% volume), cement, fly-ash

APPLICATIONS
Loadbearing and non-load-bearing walls for buildings, insulating panels, decorative elements

ENVIRONMENTAL
High recycled content, energy efficient, low maintenance, high strength-to-weight ratio

TESTS / EXAMINATIONS
All ASTM standard tests, ICC, UL, LARR and international approvals

CONTACT
Rastra Corporation
7621 East Gray Road
Scottsdale, AZ 85260
Tel: 480-443-9211 x203
www.rastra.com

SAFECRETE

AUTOCLAVED AERATED CONCRETE BLOCKS AND PANELS

SafeCrete blocks and panels, made from autoclaved aerated concrete (AAC), are noncombustible, inorganic, dimensionally accurate, and durable. The cellular structure of the material provides remarkable thermal and sound insulation. AAC products have been used in Europe since the 1920s and are among the most prevalent building materials in the world today.

SafeCrete blocks can be used for residential or small commercial construction. The light weight and workability of SafeCrete enable quick and safe installation, and the product has excellent thermal properties.

Jumbo units, which are set into place with a small crane, are recommended for larger projects. Product cost per square foot is the same, and installation is approximately fifty percent faster. Wall panels provide a fast, strong solution for very large projects with fewer openings, such as warehouses and big-box stores. The increased material cost is offset by fast installation. Floor and roof panels are used both commercially and residentially for spans up to 20 feet. These panels provide fire resistance and sound resistance between floors.

CONTENTS
70% silica (fly ash, sand, or copper mine tailings), 20% cement, 10% lime

APPLICATIONS
Structural and non-load-bearing walls (interior or exterior), firewalls, acoustic applications, elevator shafts, roofs, floors

TYPES / SIZES
Blocks from 2 × 8 × 24" (5 × 20 × 61 cm) to 12 × 24 × 40" (30.5 × 61 × 102 cm); panels from 2" × 24" × 4' (5 cm × 61 cm × 1m) to 12" × 24" × 20' (30.5 cm × 61 cm × 6m);

lintels are also available to span openings up to 18' (5.5 m)

ENVIRONMENTAL
Abundant and/or recycled raw materials, locally sourced raw materials, low embodied energy, energy efficient throughout life-cycle, non-toxic, no VOCs, closed-looped manufacturing process

TESTS / EXAMINATIONS
ER 6062, ASTM C1386, ASTM E 119, UL 919, UL 920, and others

LIMITATIONS
20' (6 m) maximum panel span, limited use below grade, not for use underwater

CONTACT
Babb Technologies, Inc.
7368 Nashville Street
Ringgold, GA 30736
Tel: 706-965-4587
www.safecrete.com

SENSITILE TERRAZZO

LIGHT-REACTIVE CONCRETE

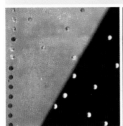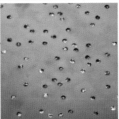

Comprised of a light-conducting matrix embedded within a substrate, SensiTiles transport light from one surface point to another by a process called Total Internal Reflection, the same principle that makes fiber optics possible. SensiTiles either respond to shadows or an active and moving light source. In the former case, SensiTiles cause any shadows that fall on their surfaces to shift. In the latter, they redirect and scatter any oncoming light. In an environment with ambient light, shadow-producing movements around a SensiTile will produce a rippling effect. In darker environments, beams of light are redirected to emerge from another part of the surface.

SensiTiles also absorb and "bleed" colors. If colored light falls on a SensiTile, echoes of that color are dispersed throughout its surface. If multiple colors are present, they become blended, rearranged, and scrambled. Because SensiTile's properties are inherent, no power is required; the light effects are created passively from external light sources, and they last as long as the material does. It is available in different substrates that each lend distinctive properties to the material. SensiTile Terrazzo is embedded in concrete to give it the durability, flexibility, and aesthetic of natural stone. The light-conducting matrix appears as a series of pixels within the concrete surface. SensiTile Terrazzo is available in a variety of standard and custom colors. (See also Scintilla, which is made entirely of acrylic.)

CONTENTS

95% concrete, 5% PMMA (polymethyl methacrylate)

APPLICATIONS

Decorative surfacing material for vertical and horizontal applications including flooring

TYPES / SIZES

4 × 4" (10 × 10 cm), 4 × 8" (10 × 20 cm), 8 × 8" (20 × 20 cm) tiles 3/4" (2 cm) thick for vertical applications, 6 × 12" (15 × 30.5 cm), 12 × 12" (30.5 × 30.5 cm), 12 × 24" (30.5 × 61 cm), 16 × 16" (40.5 × 40.5 cm) tiles 1-1/2" (3.8 cm) thick for horizontal applications; custom sizes available; custom colors available

ENVIRONMENTAL

No power required for responsive effect

CONTACT

SensiTile Systems
1604 Clay Avenue, 3rd Fl.
Detroit, MI 48211
Tel: 313-872-6314
www.sensitile.com
info@sensitile.com

SWISSPEARL

CEMENT COMPOSITE FACADE PANELS

Swisspearl panels were specially designed for the ventilated facade system. Made from a high quality cement composite, the incredibly durable panels are integrally colored with a delicate vein texture, which imparts a monolithic appearance. Swisspearl panels possess excellent color fastness, and custom colors are available on request.

CONTENTS

40% Portland cement, 30% air, 12% water, 11% pulverized limestone, 5% process fibers, 2% reinforcement fibers

APPLICATIONS

Exterior rain screen cladding, interior cladding

TYPES / SIZES

120 × 48" (304 × 1220 cm) maximum panel size

Carat integral color panel, Reflex integral gray color with pearlescent surface

ENVIRONMENTAL

Low-embodied energy manufacturing, fully recyclable

TESTS / EXAMINATIONS

ASTM 120-90, 1185-95, 84-99, 228-95, 518-98, 1308-87, G 155-00, ICC-ES number 03-10-38, various European testing reports

LIMITATIONS

Not suitable for flooring and humid rooms

CONTACT

Eternit AG Switzerland Eternitstrasse Niederurnen, CH-8867 Switzerland Tel: +41 - 55 617 13 07 www.swisspearl-architecture.com

SYNDECRETE

RECYCLED CONTENT, PRECAST CONCRETE SURFACING MATERIAL

Syndecrete is a precast concrete material developed by architect David Hertz at Syndesis, Inc., as an alternative to limited or nonrenewable natural materials such as wood and stone, as well as petroleum-based synthetic solid and laminating materials.

Syndecrete is an advanced cement-based composite using natural minerals and recycled materials as its primary ingredients. Metal shavings, plastic regrinds, recycled glass chips, and scrap wood chips are some of the postindustrial and postconsumer recycled materials incorporated into the Syndecrete matrix. These materials are used as decorative aggregates, creating a contemporary reinterpretation of the Italian tradition of terrazzo.

Syndecrete is a solid surfacing material, which provides consistency of color, texture, and aggregate throughout. Compared with conventional concrete, it has less than half the weight with twice the compressive strength.

CONTENTS

Cement, fly ash, recycled carpet fiber, perlite, sand, water, pigment, decorative aggregates

APPLICATIONS

Countertops, floor and wall tiles, planters, integral sink basins, tabletops, fixtures, accessories, sculpture, fireplace surrounds, pavers, fountains, benches, signage, coping and bollards, bathtubs, furniture

ENVIRONMENTAL

Recycled carpet fiber, fly ash, recycled decorative aggregates, no off-gassing

TESTS / EXAMINATIONS

ASTM C-19, ASTM C-39, ASTM C-48, ASTM C-501, ASTM C-642, ASTM C-1018, CTI-81-7

LIMITATIONS

Only available as a precast product, not for structural use

CONTACT

Syndesis, Inc.
2908 Colorado Avenue
Santa Monica, CA 90404
Tel: 310-829-9932
www.syndesisinc.com
inquiries@syndesisinc.com

TRANSBUOYANT CONCRETE

HIGH TENSILE STRENGTH CONCRETE

  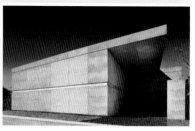

Architect Peter Jay Zweig and Monotech International, Inc., have developed an innovative, extremely fast, flexible, inexpensive, and environmentally friendly building system with a wide variety of applications. This system includes a proprietary concrete blend with performance-enhancing additives called Monocrete (which is an integral part of a double monocoque design) that Zweig terms Transbuoyant Concrete.

Unlike conventional concrete, Transbuoyant Concrete has extremely high tensile and flexural strength as well as high compression strength. The building system is durable, easily maintained, as well as earthquake, water, wind, fire, and bullet resistant. It is also extremely lightweight and easy to construct.

CONTENTS
Portland cement, sand, performance-enhancing additives

APPLICATIONS
Exterior and interior structures and surfaces

ENVIRONMENTAL
Energy efficient, thermal mass

LIMITATIONS
Structural reinforcing required for large spans

CONTACT
Monotech International, Inc.
24 Greenway Plaza
Suite 1808
Houston, TX 77046
Tel: 713-888-0507
www.monotech.com

02: MINERAL

CAMBRIA

QUARTZ SOLID SURFACE

Cambria manufactures an engineered quartzite stone comprised of ninety-three percent pure quartz crystal united with a polyester resin binder. Cambria is incredibly durable; only topaz, sapphire, and diamond are harder minerals than quartz.

Cambria quartz requires no sealing, polishing, or conditioning and costs roughly twenty percent less than stone. Using natural pigments and advanced technology allows the manufacturer of Cambria to produce a wide range of color choices not available in natural granite and marble tiles extracted from the earth.

CONTENTS
93% natural quartz, 7% polyester resin

APPLICATIONS
Kitchen and bath countertops, wall cladding, floors, fireplace surrounds, bath and shower surrounds, conference tables

TYPES / SIZES
.8, 1.2, or 1.6" (2, 3, or 4 cm) thickness;
27 colors available; edge profiling varies

ENVIRONMENTAL
No sealing or chemical maintenance required

TESTS / EXAMINATIONS
Approved by the National Sanitation Foundation International for commercial food preparation and splash zone

LIMITATIONS
For interior use only

CONTACT
Cambria
11000 West 78th Street
Suite 220
Eden Prairie, MN 55344
Tel: 866-226-2742
www.cambriausa.com
customerservice@cambria
usa.com

CONCENTRATED POWDER FORM

PROCESS THAT TURNS LIQUIDS INTO POWDER

In order to transform a liquid into powder, the liquid is mixed under pressure with a compressed gas, thereby lowering its viscosity and surface tension to such an extent that it becomes sprayable. Both liquid and gas are expanded through a nozzle, forming fine droplets. The rapid release into atmospheric pressure sets the gas free from the droplets and forms a very fine droplet spray. Simultaneously, a carrier material is added to the fine spray. The carrier particles come into contact with the liquid droplets, and free flowing powders with liquid contents of up to eighty-five percent are formed.

CONTENTS
Carrier materials: silica acid, cellulose, starch, maltodextrin, emulgator

APPLICATIONS
Food extracts, flavors, pharmaceuticals, life science products, additives

ENVIRONMENTAL
No organic solvents

CONTACT
University Bochum
VTP IB6/126
Bochum, 44780
Germany
Tel: +49 (0) 234 32 23083
www.vtp.rub.de
info@vtp.rub.de

ERLUS LOTUS

SELF-CLEANING CLAY ROOF

According to the manufacturer, Erlus Lotus is the first self-cleaning clay roof in the world. In comparison with conventional roof tiles, this system remains relatively free of dirt particles, grease deposits, soot, moss, and algae. The burned-in surface finish of this Erlus clay roof tile destroys dirt particles with the aid of sunlight, and the next rain simply washes the dirt away.

Erlus Lotus is also suitable for northern exposures, however, because the material reacts with as little as thirty percent natural daylight. The roof system achieves optimal results at temperatures of ten degrees Celsius or higher.

Erlus Lotus is based on the testing norms currently being developed for self-cleaning surfaces worldwide, based on a decomposition performance of 0.1 micrometer per day at average natural daylight, (which corresponds to a power of radiation of ten W/m2 UVA in Central Europe).

CONTENTS
100% mineral clay

APPLICATIONS
Roofs with slopes from 20° to 90°

TYPES / SIZES
E58: approx. 10 × 16.5" (26 × 42 cm); E58 MAX: approx. 11.4 × 18.3" (29 × 46.5 cm); Forma: approx. 11.6 × 18.3" (29.5 × 46.5 cm). Colors: red, brown, and black

LIMITATIONS
Not recommended for roofs with slopes less than 20°

CONTACT
Erlus AG
Hauptstrasse 106
Neufahrn, NB 84088
Germany
Tel: +49 8773 18306
www.erlus.com
info@erlus.com

DIGITAL IMAGE–FIRED CERAMIC TILE

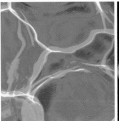

Imagine Tile, Inc., can take any two-dimensional image and incorporate it into the glaze of an incredibly vivid, commercially rated ceramic tile. Imagine Tile uses a patented process, which treats ceramic glazes like printing inks. Pure minerals and ores are ground micro-fine and suspended in a liquid to produce substances similar to printing inks. The mineral- and ore-based image is printed and coated with a refractory material that creates a glass finish. Once the tile is fired at approximately twenty-six hundred degrees Fahrenheit, the glazes fuse with the body of the tile. The result is a graphic and durable decorative tile.

Imagine Tile meets or exceeds ASTM standards for commercial floor and wall applications, and independent tests certify that the product is frostproof, UV and chemical resistant, as well as ADA compliant. Moreover, Imagine Tile possesses a surface MOH rating of seven or higher. The product is supplied with a five-year manufacturer warranty.

CONTENTS
Glazed ceramic tile

APPLICATIONS
Floors and walls in commercial and residential applications

TYPES / SIZES
8 × 8" (20 × 20 cm), 12 × 12" (30.5 × 30.5 cm), 16 × 16" (40.5 × 40.5 cm), other sizes

ENVIRONMENTAL
Glazes made from natural minerals and ores without dyes or printing inks

TESTS / EXAMINATIONS
Class 4 commercially rated ceramic tile; ADA compliant for coefficient of friction

CONTACT
Imagine Tile, Inc.
1515 Broad Street
Bloomfield, NJ 07003
Tel: 800-680-8453
www.imaginetile.com
customerservice@
imaginetile.com

NANOGEL

TRANSLUCENT SILICA AEROGEL

Manufactured by Cabot Corporation via a patented process, Nanogel is a lightweight, nanoporous material that delivers unsurpassed thermal insulation and light transmission. Comprised of nanoporous particles mixed with air, feather-light Nanogel weighs only ninety grams per liter, making it the lightest solid material in the world.

Compared with other insulation materials, Nanogel provides a superior combination of thermal and sound insulation as well as light transmission and diffusion characteristics. These benefits offer new design solutions for architects, where both maximum natural daylight levels and energy efficiency are required. Nanogel provides an R-8 insulation value for every inch of thickness, and just half an inch provides seventy-three percent light transmission with a solar heat gain coefficient of U = 0.25.

CONTENTS

97% air, 3% silica

APPLICATIONS

Translucent insulation for daylighting: translucent insulated skylights, curtain wall, roofs, walls

TYPES / SIZES

.02–.16" (.05–.4 cm) particle size, 20 nm pore size, 90% porosity

Incorporated into composite polyester, polycarbonate, and glass fenestration systems

ENVIRONMENTAL

Improved insulation performance, reduces energy consumption and HVAC costs, allows daylight to penetrate more deeply into buildings

TESTS / EXAMINATIONS

Not readily combustible substance, does not release smoke, fully hydrophobic, no UV discoloration

LIMITATIONS

The material is manufactured in a granular form and must be incorporated properly in a fenestration system by special equipment

CONTACT

Cabot Corporation
Two Seaport Lane
Suite 1300
Boston, MA 02210
Tel: 800-462-2313
www.cabot-corp.com
nanogel@cabot-corp.com

PHOTO-CAST TILES

PHOTOGRAPHIC BAS-RELIEF CERAMIC TILES

Photo-Form LLC is a tile studio that provides designers the ability to create bas-relief tiles from photographs. Utilizing their patent-pending Photo-Cast process, Photo-Form can create bas-relief ceramic tiles from any 2D image.

Photo-Cast tiles are available in sizes ranging from four inches square to eight inches square, with larger custom sizes available, and may be finished with a wide range of nontoxic glazes or bronze, brass, nickel/silver, or aluminum metal finish.

CONTENTS
Clay, non-toxic glaze (metal powder, gypsum polymer)

APPLICATIONS
Wall tiles, accents

TYPES / SIZES
4 × 4" (10 × 10 cm) up to 8 × 8" (20 × 20 cm), custom sizes available

ENVIRONMENTAL
Non-toxic

CONTACT
Photo-Form LLC
15440 North 71st Street
Suite 322
Scottsdale, AZ 85254
Tel: 888-744-3676
www.photo-form.com
sales@photo-form.com

RIVERSTONE

CARRERA MARBLE PEBBLES EMBEDDED IN CAST RESIN

Riverstone combines the beauty of Carrera marble with the transparency and uniformity of cast acrylic resin. Riverstone is ideal for interior horizontal and vertical applications and is available in a range of tinted acrylics with white pebbles or colored pebbles in a clear matrix. Riverstone is ideal for dramatic backlit applications, as the clear or tinted resin allows light to glow between each pebble.

CONTENTS
75% Carrera marble pebbles, 25% cast acrylic

APPLICATIONS
Floor tiles, wall tiles, tabletops, counters, bartops

TYPES / SIZES
12 × 12 × 1/2" (30.5 × 30.5 × 1.3 cm) thick tiles, 32 × 72 × 1/4" (81 × 183 × .6 cm) slabs

LIMITATIONS
Tiles must be trimmed with a wet saw, material is not fire rated, not for exterior use

CONTACT
Robin Reigi, Inc.
48 West 21st Street
New York, NY 10010
Tel: 212-924-5558
www.robin-reigi.com
info@robin-reigi.com

SPHELAR

SPHERICAL MICRO SOLAR CELLS

  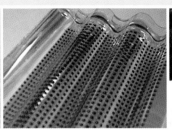 

Sphelar is currently the most versatile photovoltaic (PV) technology in the market. Made from single crystalline silicon, it has the durability and reliability of conventional silicon-based PV, yet the micro spherical shape of cells makes it lightweight and extremely pliable. Some of Sphelar's unique features are: 1) high photo-electric conversion efficiency, 2) omni-directionality, 3) module transparency, 4) configurability in series or parallel circuits, and 5) fits almost any shape and size module.

Sphelar technology is ideal for building integrated photovoltaics (BIPV). Sphelar modules can be easily integrated with curtain walls, windows, roofing materials, canopies, etc. Sphelar is also ideal for ubiquitous computing and electronics, because the micro spherical particles are smaller and more effective than conventional photovoltaics.

CONTENTS
Single crystalline silicon

APPLICATIONS
Building integrated photovoltaics (BIPV), portable electronic devices

ENVIRONMENTAL
Renewable energy source, less embodied energy, and fewer materials than conventional PVs

LIMITATIONS
ISO 9001

CONTACT
Kyosemi Corporation
949-2 Ebisu-Cho
Fushimi-ku
Kyoto, 612-8201
Japan
Tel +206-230-6448
www.kyosemi.co.jp
info-ussolar@kyosemi.
co.jp

SURFACE

FINE AGGREGATE ARCHITECTURAL WALL COATINGS

Surface offers a collection of five unique finishes, which combine raw materials like silica, crystal, and titanium flakes with quality acrylics to develop high performance wall coatings.

Gobi appears like suede: it is soft, lush, yet firm and smooth. Flint is a grainy translucent finish with particles that have been filtered and screened down to a medium-sized grain. Spar resembles frosted parchment. Crush has the appearance of crushed ice, blended from marble particles of a uniform density. Po is a powdery, chalk-like finish that has a pure matte texture.

Surface products are composed of silica-based aggregates, powdered marble dust, and tints suspended in an acrylic polymer medium. These finishes are tolerant of common spills and stains such as dirt, shoe scuffs, pen ink, graphite, or food. Soiled finishes may be cleaned with mild non-abrasive household cleansers.

Surface finishes generally require a two-step process: 1) cover substrate with Surface tinted scratch coat, 2) trowel on Surface finish coat in two passes

CONTENTS
Marble, plaster, and silica powders with colored pigments

APPLICATIONS
Walls and ceilings

TYPES / SIZES
Gobi, Flint, Spar, Crush, Po

ENVIRONMENTAL
Low volatile organic compounds, water soluble

LIMITATIONS
Not for exterior use, do not use abrasive chemical cleaners

CONTACT
Robin Reigi Inc. with Surface Interiors
48 West 21st Street
New York, NY 10010
Tel: 212-924-5558
www.robin-reigi.com
info@robin-reigi.com

ARCHITECTURAL TERRA COTTA FACADE PANELS AND ELEMENTS

Today, masonry is used in building facades more often for its durability and weather protection than for its traditional qualities as a load-bearing material. NBK Keramik's Terrart is a suspended rain-screen facade system made from terra-cotta. Terrart consists of large, precisely crafted ceramic elements designed to be ventilated from within the wall cavity. In this way, the system is designed to shed water while allowing the cavity to breathe, thus maintaining a consistent air pressure between the cavity and the exterior.

CONTENTS
100% natural clays

APPLICATIONS
Exterior facade and interior wall cladding

TYPES / SIZES
4 × 23.5" (10 × 60 cm) to 23.5 × 63" (60 × 160 cm) panels, custom baguette sizes up to 57" (145 cm)

ENVIRONMENTAL
100% recyclable, increases building's energy efficiency

TESTS / EXAMINATIONS
ASTM C 67, ASTM C 126, DIN EN ISO 10545 2, 4, 8, and 12

CONTACT
NBK Keramik GmbH & Co.
Reeser Str. 235
Emmerich am Rhein, 46446
Germany
Tel: +46 2822 8111 -0
www.nbk.de
info@nbk.de

ULTRAPERFORMING MATERIAL

TRANSPARENT CERAMICS

TRANSPARENT HIGH-STRENGTH OXIDE CERAMICS

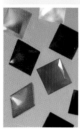

Translucent alumina ceramics have exhibited low mechanical properties and a low in-line transmission of unscattered light (less than fifteen percent) because of their coarse micro-structures (greater than 20 µm).

New transparent corundum ceramics avoid these shortcomings and can be manufactured with complex (even hollow) shapes and with a four-point bending strength of six hundred to seven hundred megapascals and a macrohardness HV10 greater than 20 GPa. The in-line transmission of transparent ceramics is close to sixty percent in visible light and approaches the theoretical limit in the infrared range. An even higher visible light transmission (greater than eighty percent at one millimeter thickness) is enabled by new submicrometer spinel, which has a macrohardness of HV10 = 14.5 GPa.

Faceted colored gemstones of about one and a half carats have been manufactured with a polycrystalline sub-µm microstructure of transparent ceramics, and filters have been manufactured for optical applications with the same material. Future applications include superstrong and heat-resistant windows as well as transparent armor.

CONTENTS
Alumina (Al2O3) or
spinel (MgO.Al2O3)

APPLICATIONS
Transparent armor,
windows (for corrosive,
high temperature or wear-
related environments, IR
windows), burners for
discharge lamps, orthodon-
tic products, colored filters,
gemstones

TYPES / SIZES
Flat or complex shapes
up to 4" (10 cm)

CONTACT
Fraunhofer IKTS
Winterbergstrasse 28
Dresden, 01277
Germany
Tel: +49 351 2553 519
www.ikts.fraunhofer.de

HONEYCOMB-REINFORCED LIGHTWEIGHT STONE PANELS

Ultra-Lite Stone Panels combine the aerospace technology of aluminum honeycomb structures with the natural purity of granite, marble, or limestone. Ultra-Lite Stone is particularly suitable for interior or exterior applications typically considered weight- or cost-prohibitive.

The honeycomb-reinforced panels present the beauty of natural stone yet eliminate its fragile, brittle properties, since the reinforcing gives the panels high impact and flexural strength. For instance, Ultra-Lite Stone can resist up to sixty times more impact than three-centimeter-thick solid granite. These panels can also be flexed, making them ideal for seismic locations.

Ultra-Lite Stone is impervious to water penetration, even with open-structured stones such as travertine. The fiber-reinforced epoxy skin, located directly behind the stone, provides a waterproof barrier that eliminates the need for a secondary layer of protection.

Ultra-Lite Stone Panels are available in nearly unlimited choices of natural marble, granite, and limestone from quarries throughout the world. Several finishes are available, including polished, honed, sandblasted, flamed, antiqued, and bush-hammered surfaces.

CONTENTS
Stone facing, aluminum honeycomb, fiber-reinforced epoxy resin

APPLICATIONS
Exterior and interior wall cladding, ceilings, and soffits

TYPES / SIZES
4 × 8' (1.2 × 2.4 m) or 5 × 8' (1.5 × 2.4 m) standard size, 5 × 10' (1.5 × 3 m) maximum size; 9/16" (1.4 cm) or 15/16" (2.4 cm) thickness

ENVIRONMENTAL
80% less material than traditional stone construction, lightweight

TESTS / EXAMINATIONS
ASTM E-84, ASTM E-695, others

CONTACT
Stone Panels, Inc.
100 South Royal Lane
Coppell, TX 75019
Tel: 800-328-6275
www.stonepanels.com

UTI & INNI

TEXTURED PORCELAIN TILE

Italy's Gruppo Majorca has crafted a new line of porcelain tiles in five colors and five atypical textures for use in vertical and horizontal applications. The tiles have integral color, and their edges may be left natural or edge-ground for minimal joint lines.

CONTENTS
100% porcelain

APPLICATIONS
Floor and wall tiling

TYPES / SIZES
6.1 × 6.1" (15.5 × 15.5 cm),
12.4 × 12.4" (31.5 × 31.5
cm), 18.3 × 18.3" (46.5 ×
46.5 cm), 18.7 × 18.7"
(47.5 × 47.5 cm)

CONTACT
Gruppo Majorca
Via del Bosco 26
Scandiano (RE), 42019
Italy
www.majorca.it
majorca@majorca.it

03: **METAL**

AEGIS HYPOSURFACE

ENVIRONMENTALLY RESPONSIVE ARCHITECTURAL SURFACE

Designed by Mark Goulthorpe of dECOi Architects, the Aegis project consists of an interactive mechanical surface that deforms in real-time based on various environmental stimuli, including the sounds and movements of people, weather, and electronic information.

The Hyposurface is comprised by a matrix of actuators, which are given positional information via a highly efficient bus system as well as an array of electronic sensors used to trigger a variety of mathematical deployment programs. The Hyposurface effectively elevates a highly responsive pneumatic mechanical system to a level of articulate and fluid control through its interception by a highly performative digital control.

dECOi Architects' goal for the Aegis Hyposurface is "to utterly radicalize architecture by announcing the possibility of dynamic form, and to then explore the cultural possibilities afforded by this new medium. It is, of course, a harbinger of nanotechnology—the intersection of information and matter itself."

CONTENTS
Metallic surfaces, 896 pneumatic pistons, electronic sensors, computer, software

APPLICATIONS
Interactive art, feature wall

CONTACT
MIT Department of Architecture
77 Massachusetts Avenue
7-337
Cambridge, MA 02139
Tel: 617-452-3061
www.sial.rmit.edu.au/
Projects/Aegis_
Hyposurface.php
mg_decoi@mit.edu

CORRUGATED ANODIZED ALUMINUM SHEETS

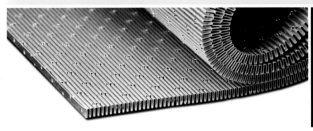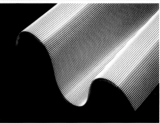

Aero consists of tightly corrugated anodized aluminum sheets that are flexible and formable. Crisp, exacting folds characterize each sheet and cast deep shadows that contribute to the dimensionality of the material. Variations in thickness, depth, and return edges (either rounded or square) produce unique designs. Some panel types include precision-engineered perforations.

Aero is ideal for a breadth of interior applications, whether the visual impact desired is an emphasis on geometric compositions or fluid curves. The matte silver anodized finish is a natural complement to other materials.

CONTENTS

Formed silver anodized aluminum (alloy #3003)

APPLICATIONS

Retail displays and fixtures, electronic components, home/office accessories, furniture insets, column covers, counter facings, wainscoting, base mold-ings, trim pieces, architec-tural accents, signage, and lighting

TYPES / SIZES

45.7 × 17.7 × 0.2" or 0.3" (45 × 116 × .4 or .7 cm); distinctive perforation patterns available

ENVIRONMENTAL

High recycled content; 100% recyclable

LIMITATIONS

Not recommended for exterior use

CONTACT

Forms+Surfaces
6395 Cindy Lane
Carpinteria, CA 93013
Tel: 800-451-0410
www.forms-surfaces.com
marketing@forms-surfaces.com

MULTIDIMENSIONAL PRODUCT

ALGORHYTHMS

ALGORITHMICALLY DERIVED METAL SYSTEMS

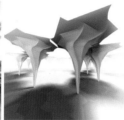

Milgo/Bufkin can bend complex shapes in metal, providing solutions to the most demanding problems. These shapes are economical alternatives to extrusions and roll forming.

Just as our genetic code permits each of us to be unique, so too AlgoRhythm technology generates a wide range of unique forms from its genetic code. Milgo/Bufkin's process offers a wide range of curvilinear structures with fluid movements mirroring the flows of nature. Material flows under its own weight and other forces according to morphologic laws that pertain more to fluid motion than to static objects. By freeing the elements of construction from their rigid geometries, AlgoRhythm technology unfolds infinite opportunities to model a new architecture. The undulating look of these structures results from the behavior of sheet metal under force. The forms are nondeformational, thereby maintaining the integrity of the metal.

Dr. Haresh Lalvani, architect-morphologist and inventor of these new forms, says that Algo-Rhythms proceed from the bottom-up: columns, walls, and ceilings. The first series of products introduced here are based on morphologically structured information (meta architecture, genomic architecture) that permits endless variations on a theme by manipulating the morphological genome.

CONTENTS
Steel or other sheet metals

APPLICATIONS
Architectural exteriors and interiors, as well as stand-alone structures

ENVIRONMENTAL
Substantial efficiencies in manufacturing processes due to mass-customization

TESTS / EXAMINATIONS
Tested for strength and deformation

CONTACT
Milgo/Bufkin
68 Lombardy Street
Brooklyn, NY 11222
Tel: 718-388-6476
www.milgo-bufkin.com/algorhythms
milgomail@aol.com

ALKEMI

RECYCLED ALUMINUM SOLID SURFACE

Alkemi is a recycled composite material composed of a minimum of sixty percent postindustrial scrap aluminum and polymeric resins for use as a solid surface material. It is strong, durable, and exquisite to the eye. Alkemi offers a fresh and innovative alternative to the traditional commercial options such as plastic laminate, stone, and glass. Alkemi may be sanded and buffed to a matte or a high-gloss surface, and the material can be cut and shaped using conventional woodworking tools.

CONTENTS
Aluminum, polymeric resin

APPLICATIONS
Countertops, cabinetry, bar fronts, horizontal or vertical interior surfaces

TYPES / SIZES
36 × 96" (91.5 × 244 cm) and 36 × 120" (91.5 × 305 cm) standard panel sizes, 1/2 and 3/4" (1.3 and 1.9 cm) thick; textured or honed finish; a variety of colors available

ENVIRONMENTAL
At least 60% postindustrial content

TESTS / EXAMINATIONS
ASTM D256, D570, D648, D790, D792, D2583

CONTACT
Renewed Materials LLC
PO Box 55
Cabin John, MD 20818
Tel: 301-320-0042
www.renewed
materials.com
info@renewed
materials.com

ALUMINUM FOAM

Alulight aluminum foam was designed to combine attributes such as high stiffness, low weight, and high energy absorption—qualities that enable aluminum foam to qualify for specific requirements within the automotive, aviation, railway, and engine-building industries. Aluminum foam is also suitable for architecture and interior design applications, where sound absorption, electromagnetic shielding, structural damping, flame resistance, or decorative surfacing is required.

Alulight is distinctive for its light weight (roughly five times lighter than pure aluminum) as well as its superior mechanical characteristics. Alulight is available in the form of panels and can also be produced to the customer's specifications in complex moldings.

Alulight GmbH produces metal foams and their precursor materials as well as powder metal products.

CONTENTS
99.7% aluminum alloy

APPLICATIONS
EM-shielding, resonance limiting, acoustic noise reduction, crash absorption, aesthetic applications

TYPES / SIZES
24.5 × 24.5 × .4–1.4" (62.5 × 62.5 × 1–3.5 cm), custom sizes available

ENVIRONMENTAL
100% recyclable, efficient use of material, flame resistant

CONTACT
Alulight GmbH
A-5282 Ranshofen
Lach, 22 Germany
Tel: +0043-7722-645640
www.alulight.com
office@alulight.com

ALUMA FLOOR

N° 055400-001

ALUMINUM FLOOR TILES AND PANELS

Aluma Floor is a machined-aluminum floor system. Its high-tolerance prefabrication allows for precision-fitting panels, eliminating the need for grouting. Aluma Floor panels are affixed with adhesive to a suitable subfloor without exposed fasteners. The panels have hand-beveled edges, are available in three hand finishes, and are clear-coat anodized for ease of maintenance. Custom sizes are also available.

CONTENTS
Recycled aluminum

APPLICATIONS
Flooring, paneling

TYPES / SIZES
24 × 24" (61 × 61 cm),
24 × 48" (61 × 122 cm), 3/16"
(.5 cm) thick, custom sizes
available

ENVIRONMENTAL
Made from recycled
postindustrial content,
completely recyclable

TESTS / EXAMINATIONS
ASTM 0.752

LIMITATIONS
Not for exterior use

CONTACT
Power Stretch, Inc.
740 Annoreno Drive
Addison, IL 60101
Tel: 630-628-0226
www.aluminumfloors.com
franalumafloor@sbc
global.net

BODY INDEX

BIOMORPHICALLY DERIVED CHAIR

Designed by Sean Ahlquist, Body Index is intended to capture multiple body positions within a single form. The design utilizes software technology that generates physical fabric simulations defined by a geometrical surface and assigned certain cloth characteristics such as stiffness, stretching, and weight.

Different forces, actions, and collisions act upon the geometry. The initial state of the geometry is affected by gravity as well as the direct control over one edge of the surface to activate a waving motion. The surface then engages a human figure as it moves through different body positions, and the software generates the reactions to the dynamic forces. The surface is captured at a certain moment within the animated process and fixed for use in fabricating the built piece.

The digital geometry is used in creating laser-cut profiles of the core of the chair surface. These profiles are cut in varying thicknesses of plywood, dependent on the complexity of the curvature of the surface. The core is clad in strips of leather, and the base profile is laser cut and rolled, according to the data retrieved from the digital model.

CONTENTS
Steel base, leather-clad
plywood core

APPLICATIONS
Furniture

TYPES / SIZES
48 × 24 × 30"
(122 × 61 × 76 cm)

CONTACT
Proces2
1663 Mission Street,
Mezzanine
San Francisco, CA 94110
Tel: 415-252-5011
www.proces2.com

BONDED METAL

LIGHTWEIGHT METAL SHEETS WITH DURABLE CASTINGS

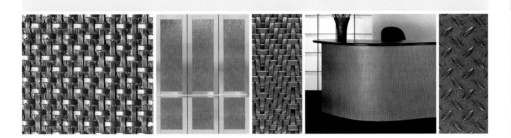

Bonded Metal is the product of a unique technology that casts metal granules within a durable FRP matrix. Advanced mold-making techniques assure precise reproduction of fine detail in the original patterned surface. The result is a lightweight but extremely durable casting with the character and appearance of solid metal.

Bonded Metal is available in a wide collection of patterns and a variety of finishes. The product can be specified for any interior application where requirements include visual richness and exceptional resistance to wear.

CONTENTS
Cast metal granules in an FRP matrix

APPLICATIONS
Interior applications including walls, doors, elevators, and accents

ENVIRONMENTAL
Long life cycle

LIMITATIONS
Not recommended for exterior use

CONTACT
Forms+Surfaces
6395 Cindy Lane
Carpinteria, CA 93013
Tel: 800-451-0410
www.forms-surfaces.com
marketing@forms-surfaces.com

CELLSCREEN

DECORATIVE ALUMINUM SCREEN

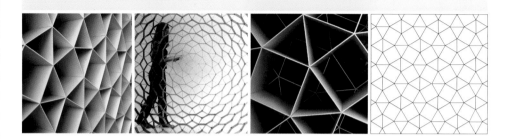

The Cellscreen is a simple mathematical honeycomb panel crafted from crisp, lightweight aluminum. It is a cellular filter structure that explores rhythm, repetition, and sequence. Intending to achieve visual density and decorative effect with a minimum of means, designers at Korban Flaubert generated the Cellscreen from the simplest geometry, using a single line length and a repeated five-way joint.

Inspired by decorative patterns in Islamic architecture, mathematical sequences, and patterns in nature, the Cellscreen is a product that possesses an intensity of decorative detail yet is produced using industrial processes.

CONTENTS
Anodized aluminum

APPLICATIONS
Decorative filter screen for any interior

TYPES / SIZES
71 × 71 × 4" (180 × 180 × 10 cm) or custom sizes

CONTACT
Korban Flaubert
8/8-10 Burrows Road
St. Peters, NSW 2044
Australia
Tel: +61 2 95576136
www.korbanflaubert.com.au

CONSTRUCTIV PON

Metal

RAPID-CONSTRUCTION ARCHITECTURAL SYSTEM

Constructiv PON is a rapid-construction system that employs connectors and rods that are joined using magnetic push-fit connections. It can be assembled and disassembled easily and quickly without any need for tools, and diagonal braces are simply inserted into position.

Light and graceful in appearance, Constructiv PON is nevertheless extremely stable. It is a complete architectural system for use in trade fairs, displays, or shop systems—wherever versatile spatial structures are needed on a temporary basis. The connectors permit installation of all kinds of panels (textile, plastic, solid, glass) without using tools. Thanks to its slender rods and compact connectors, Constructiv PON has a low transport weight and loading volume.

The basic Constructiv PON system is orthogonal, but multiple-angled construction is possible when it is used with connectors from Constructiv Telvis I.

ULTRAPERFORMING PRODUCT

CONTENTS
Precision-cast stainless steel (connectors) and high-strength aluminum (rods)

APPLICATIONS
Temporary architecture

TYPES / SIZES
Basic axis dimensions: 39 and 47" (98 and 120 cm); connectors 1.3 × 1.3 × 1.3" (3.4 × 3.4 × 3.4 cm); panels between .04 and .79" (.1 and 2 cm)

ENVIRONMENTAL
Minimal use of materials, long life, reusable system

CONTACT
Burkhardt Leitner Constructiv GmbH & Co. KG Blumenstrasse 36 Stuttgart, 70182 Germany Tel: 416-251-1600 or + 0049-711-25588-13 www.burkhardtleitner.de

EXOGRID

TRIANGULATED METAL COMPOSITE FRAME

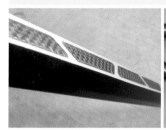  

ExoGrid is a technology that was initially developed to improve the performance of high-end bicycle frames. In this application, the tubes of a typical triangular space frame are made up of various tubes, each with a different diameter and wall thickness. The goal is to achieve a certain function level while maintaining the lowest possible weight, the highest possible stiffness and strength, the best energy efficiency, and the most desirable aesthetic appearance.

ExoGrid allowed VyaTek Sports to optimize these attributes by reducing the weight of a standard titanium tube through a laser machining operation, and then fusing an inner composite tube to the titanium tube through a high pressure/temperature operation. The resulting tube is lighter due to the rule of mixtures of the various metal/composite materials, but also has a higher torsional stiffness (GJ profile), creating a frame that has better energy transmission.

Due to the unique "tunability" of the hybrid tube design, the bending characteristics of the tubes are also softer, thus improving the resilience of the material. The contrasting look of the carbon and metal also creates a stunning look.

CONTENTS
Titanium (or other metal), graphite (or other advanced composite material)

APPLICATIONS
High-performance metal-based structures: bicycles, sports equipment, motorcycles, ultra-light automobiles

ENVIRONMENTAL
High strength-to-weight ratio

CONTACT
VyaTek Sports
8214 East Sharon Drive
Scottsdale, AZ 85260
Tel: 480-998-2046
www.vyatek.com
info@vyatek.com

CAST METAL VERTICAL WALL SURFACING

Gagecast is a cast metal surfacing appropriate for vertical applications consisting of metal patterns that feature high luster, pattern depth, durability, and cost-effective installation. Gagecast is composed of metal particles dispersed throughout the casting rather than an applied topical application. Gagecast's patented process allows the casting to be manufactured with a choice of installer-friendly substrates and three distinct installation systems (Adhesive, Z-Bar, and Extrusion), thereby providing the specifier versatility for the intended application. Certain designs are either applicable or can be adapted to satisfy the thickness requirement for elevator doors.

Gagecast offers twenty-five standard designs, and custom designs are welcomed. All designs can be specified in a number of single metal finishes; however, most designs can also be specified in a combination of two finishes. Factory-cut panels to match field dimensions and/or shop drawings are available. Gagecast is typically protected by a durable clear topcoat to prevent oxidation, and it is also available uncoated to promote a natural patina. Black (BP) and Verdi Gris (VG) patinas are also available options.

CONTENTS
80% metal powders, 20% binding resin

APPLICATIONS
Dimensional cast metal suitable for vertical surfacing

TYPES / SIZES
4 × 8' (1.2 × 2.4 m) sheets for adhesive application or panels for use with Gage extrusion system

ENVIRONMENTAL
ISO 14001 manufacturing methods

TESTS / EXAMINATIONS
ASTM E 84 Class B

LIMITATIONS
Not for exterior or curved panel applications

CONTACT
The Gage Corporation, Int.
803 South Black River Street
Sparta, WI 54656
Tel: 800-786-4243
www.gagevertical
surfacing.com
gage@centurytel.net

MULTIDIMENSIONAL PRODUCT

GEOMETRIX

LIGHTWEIGHT RECYCLED METAL CEILING PANELS

Geometrix Metal Ceiling Panels add an entirely new dimension to metal ceiling design. The lightweight aluminum panels are offered in a variety of profiles and depths to create highly distinctive 3D ceiling treatments featuring articulated planes, juxtaposed angles, and other geometric perspectives.

Geometrix panel profiles can be combined to create intentional patterns or installed randomly to add dimensional variety to ceiling space. They can be used in combination with other ceiling panels from USG Interiors or can be designed to incorporate negative space for truly unique ceiling designs.

An optional Compasso edge trim may be added to the ceiling to create a more finished appearance at exposed edges.

CONTENTS
Pretreated, prepainted recycled aluminum

APPLICATIONS
Interior ceilings

TYPES / SIZES
2 × 2' (.6 × .6 m) panels designed for 9/16" (1.4 cm) narrow profile and 15/16" (2.4 cm) standard suspension systems; four profiles with various depths; solid metal or five acoustically backed perforated patterns; two standard colors (white and silver satin) with custom colors available on request

ENVIRONMENTAL
Contains 90% recycled content

LIMITATIONS
For interior use only

CONTACT
USG Interiors, Inc.
125 South Franklin Street
Chicago, IL 60606
Tel: 800-874-4968
www.usg.com
usg4you@usg.com

WOVEN METAL FABRICS

  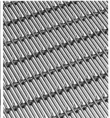 

Woven metal fabrics have been developed for use as decorative and functional design elements in architecture. The French National Library in Paris was the first architectural project where GKD, in cooperation with French architect Dominique Perrault, succeeded in systematically implementing metal meshes in a building in various ways and applications. Since then, this development has continued worldwide.

For decades, GKD has manufactured metal fabrics for industrial applications in filtration and separation technologies and the process belt sector. At first, it was their visual attractiveness that made metal fabrics suitable for the architecture and design sector. During the continuous product development, it became clear that metal fabrics also have considerable technical advantages, which are extremely relevant in the field of architecture. Today, there are a wide range of fabric samples, with weaving widths up to twenty-six feet.

Woven metal fabrics may be used as partition elements, projection screens, and acoustic scrims appropriate for public buildings, opera houses, and concert halls.

CONTENTS
Stainless steel, copper, brass, bronze, and aluminum

APPLICATIONS
Exterior facades, wall coverings, ceilings, column coverings, sunshades, partition screens, balustrades

TYPES / SIZES
Maximum panel size
110 × 26' (33.5 × 8 m)

ENVIRONMENTAL
100% recyclable, reduces solar radiation when used as a sunshade

CONTACT
GKD-USA, Inc.
825 Chesapeake Drive
Cambridge, MD 21613
Tel: 410-221-0542
www.gkdmetalfabrics.com
sales@gkdmetalfabrics.com

ULTRAPERFORMING MATERIAL

GREENSCREEN

RECYCLED STEEL-LANDSCAPE TRELLIS SYSTEM

Greenscreen is a landscape trellis system for fencing, wall-mounted applications, or freestanding enclosures. When combined with a variety of climbing vines, Greenscreen becomes a "living wall" that can provide privacy, shading and cooling, security and spatial definition, and acts as an effective antigraffiti treatment. The main component of this modular system is a 3D welded wire trellis panel, which is manufactured in Southern California from recycled-content galvanized steel wire.

CONTENTS
Recycled galvanized steel wire

APPLICATIONS
Vertical landscaping elements for wall mounted applications, fencing, screening, and freestanding enclosures

TYPES / SIZES
Standard panels are 4 × 6, 8, 10, 12 or 14' (1.2 m × 1.8, 2.4, 3, 3.7, or 4.3 m) with custom sizes available in 2" (5 cm) increments up to 4 × 14' (1.2 × 4.3 m)

ENVIRONMENTAL
Recycled content, landscaped walls increase energy efficiency

CONTACT
Impac International
11445 Pacific Avenue
Fontana, CA 92337
Tel: 800-450-3494
www.greenscreen.com
sales@greenscreen.com

RIB-REINFORCED THIN-WALL STRUCTURES

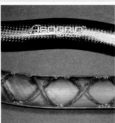

When a thin-wall structure is loaded in compression, it eventually reaches a point of instability, where the wall buckles out of plane. This buckling results in a loss in stiffness, which accelerates exponentially because of increased bending moment. This phenomena is referred to as an "exponential decay function"; once a thin-wall structure starts to become unstable, it quickly fails unless the load is removed.

Howard Lindsay with VyaTek Sports developed IsoGrid in order to avoid this phenomena and to help product designers lower the weight of products by making thin-wall structures even thinner. The technology incorporates a continuous fiber-reinforced array of raised ribs, which are integrated into thin-wall structures in order to enhance structural integrity, greatly decreasing the chances of collapse.

CONTENTS
99% carbon fiber; 1% zylon

APPLICATIONS
Wheelchairs, ultra-light motor vehicles, sports equipment; any weight-sensitive thin-wall structure prone to buckling-related failure

TYPES / SIZES
0.040–0.150" (.1–.38 cm) diameter raised ribs

ENVIRONMENTAL
High strength-to-weight ratio

CONTACT
VyaTek Sports
8214 East Sharon Drive
Scottsdale, AZ 85260
Tel: 480-998-2046
www.vyatek.com
info@vyatek.com

ULTRAPERFORMING MATERIAL

MEMBRANE

STEEL MESH CHAISE LONGUE

Membrane is a steel chaise longue that is virtually transparent. A single thread of stainless steel is wound in a continuous spiral, and then a force of twenty-eight tons is applied slowly and strategically to create its simple supine form. Surface and structure are one: there is no chassis; it is a true and organic monocoque.

Membrane is made of pure stainless steel with no applied coatings or finishing products, meaning that it is suitable for exterior use. A marine-grade variation is available for poolside applications.

CONTENTS
Electropolished spiral-wound, resistance-welded stainless steel mesh

APPLICATIONS
Seating

TYPES / SIZES
71 × 31.5 × 25.5"
(180 × 80 × 65 cm)

CONTACT
Korban Flaubert
8/8-10 Burrows Road
St. Peters, NSW 2044
Australia
Tel: +61 2 95576136
www.korbanflaubert.com.au

META-COAT

METAL-PLATING PROCESS FOR PLASTICS

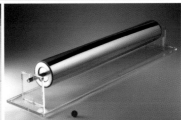

The Meta-Coat process allows many metals to be replaced by metal-plated plastics, thus saving energy and operating expenses. When print-industry rollers are made of carbon fiber–reinforced plastic (CFRP), for example, approximately up to seventy-five percent of energy can be saved over using conventional steel rollers. In the automotive industry, fuel is saved directly by reducing the weight of the vehicles.

The Meta-Coat process first involves microstructuring the surface of the base material. After activation of the surface, the first conductive metal layer is deposited on the plastic by a chemical process. A subsequent electroplated metal layer reinforces the chemically produced layer. Thus, metals like nickel, copper, tin, gold, or silver can be added in an economic way. Due to excellent adhesion, mechanical processing, such as turning or drilling through metal layers into the plastic material, is possible.

CONTENTS
Nickel, phosphorus, and additional metals based on the application

APPLICATIONS
Housings (EMC, shielding), carbon fiber reinforced plastics (CFRP), glass fiber reinforced plastics (GFRP), rapid prototyping, and rapid tooling

TYPES / SIZES
6–150 µm layer thickness; .08" (.2 cm) maximum thickness

ENVIRONMENTAL
Optimizes use of materials; increases energy efficiency

CONTACT
Imecotec GmbH
Industriestraße 1a
Siegen, 57076 Germany
Tel: +0271-3130 540
www.imecotec.de
info@ahc-surface.com

MICROTRUSS

SANDWICHED PERIODIC CELLULAR MATERIALS

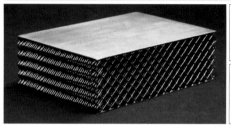  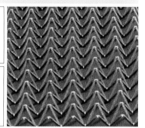

CMI develops and manufactures structures based on periodic cellular material (PCM) technology that are incredibly light, strong, multifunctional, efficient at heat exchange, and versatile due to their design and material flexibility. CMI's PCM is now being incorporated into advanced applications that require structural support, armor protection, and thermal management as well as a combination of these functions. These structures' multifunctionality provides innovations such as enhanced fuel cell performance, increased payloads for spacecraft, as well as increased durability for military vehicles.

CMI's periodic cellular materials are comprised of a lightweight core sandwiched between two face sheets. CMI utilizes a wide variety of designs for its proprietary structures such as pyramidal and tetrahedral configurations, collectively referred to as Microtruss. Both the core and face sheets are manufactured from proven and established commercial materials, employing standard metallurgical processes in a variety of designs, densities, and metals suited to the specifications of an application.

CONTENTS
Titanium, aluminum, copper, steel, stainless steel, others depending on application

APPLICATIONS
Load-bearing structures, blast and/or ballistic protection, heat transfer

ENVIRONMENTAL
Efficient use of material, fuel and energy savings

CONTACT
Cellular Materials International, Inc. (CMI)
2 Boar's Head Lane
Charlottesville, VA 22903
Tel: 434-977-1405
www.cellularmaterials.com
info@cellularmaterials.com

PRE-ASSEMBLED, MOVEABLE, FULL-HEIGHT PARTITIONS

ULTRAPERFORMING PRODUCT

Waste resulting from the traditional construction, demolition, and renovation of buildings contributes to twenty-five to thirty-three percent of the total waste stream in North America, and fifteen percent of that amount is drywall waste. Overburdened landfills and the consumption of virgin resources are significant problems that influenced Haworth to develop a sustainable moveable wall solution for the office market.

Unitized construction allows Haworth's moveable panels to be relocated without disassembly for faster installation and reconfiguration timelines. The various available wall coverings and finishes are made from rapidly renewable and recycled materials. The moveable wall system is also designed for disassembly, refinishing, and/or recycling at the end of its lifecycle in order to support Haworth's "cradle to cradle" design rationale.

State-of-the-art materials such as luminescent glass and light-refracting films are also available and bring daylight farther into the office interior, thus reducing typical lighting loads.

CONTENTS

Doors: 33% aluminum, 63% glass, 3% steel, 1% plastic

Glass panels: 27% aluminum, 69% glass, 3% steel, 1% plastic

Solid panels: 72% gypsum, 14% aluminum, 5% steel, 4% recycled wallcovering, 2% plastic. Available finishes: 100% recycled art glass (Joel Berman Glass Studios), 100% recycled wood pulp wallcoverings, 100% recycled aluminum, 100% recycled cotton insulation. Rapid growth veneers from bamboo and Lyptus are available

APPLICATIONS

Office interiors

TYPES / SIZES

Doors: 24–48" (61 × 122 cm) (swing and sliding barn doors); solid panels: 6–60" (15–152.5 cm) wide at 1/16" (.16 cm) increments up to 144" (366 cm) high

ENVIRONMENTAL

Minimizes waste, low VOCs, minimizes office churn, utilizes rapidly renewable and recycled products, disassembly and recycling program

TESTS / EXAMINATIONS

Meets North American model building code requirements

LIMITATIONS

Not for exterior use, not for fire-rated assemblies or clean room environments

CONTACT

Haworth
10 Smed Lane
Calgary, Alberta
Canada
Tel: 403-203-6000
www.haworth.com

PROTOTYPE

CARBON FIBER FURNITURE COLLECTION DESIGNED BY GIOVANNI PAGNOTTA

Prior to initiating a project, Giovanni Pagnotta always asks himself: If there were no rules, no limits, no budgets, if all that mattered were the truest, best design you could create, how would it manifest itself? In the case of his carbon-fiber furniture collection, the high strength-to-weight ratio of the material allows for incredibly thin cross sections. In the words of Pagnotta, "the old rules become warped; design becomes gesture, calligraphic, reduced to its lowest common denominator."

Pagnotta introduced the collection in 2002, calling it Prototype. The Prototype series demonstrates the extent to which a high-performance material can redefine process and aesthetics. The cornerstone piece, the Z5 chair, is constructed entirely of carbon fiber. The chair weighs approximately fourteen pounds and has been load-tested in excess of three thousand pounds with no indication of impending structural failure. It has a varying sectional thickness of less than 0.5 inches at its foot, and it tapers to 0.13 inches at its seat back. The chair is constructed of layered plies of carbon fiber, and it has between ten and forty individual plies between its thinnest and thickest points.

CONTENTS
Carbon fiber; in some cases foam and leather

APPLICATIONS
Furniture

TYPES / SIZES
Z5 chair

ENVIRONMENTAL
Highly efficient strength-to-weight ratio

CONTACT
Giovanni Pagnotta
458 Halstead Avenue #1
Mamaroneck, NY 10543
Tel: 914-309-0720
giovannipagnotta.com

PROTRUDE, FLOW

MAGNETIC FLUID ART

Magnetic fluid is a black liquid that is made by dissolving ferro-magnetic micro-powder in a solvent such as oil or water. The powder retains its magnetic properties even in its liquid state, which allows for the creation of complex, organic shapes that cannot be rendered with regular magnetic sand.

Inspired by the transformational nature of this material, Tokyo-based artists Sachiko Kodama and Minako Takeno developed an interactive installation entitled *Protrude, Flow*, in which magnetic fluid responds to the volume of viewers' voices by adopting 3D forms. The image of this dynamic exchange is projected on a gigantic screen, where the magnetic fluid resembles steep mountains, pliable organic shapes, and flowing particle streams.

Kodama and Takeno have devised several other works such as "Pulsate," "Equilibrium Point," and "Waves and Sea Urchins," all of which change dynamically based on the qualities of ambient noise, light, and temperature in their environments.

CONTENTS
Magnetic Fluid: 61–71% synthetic hydrocarbon, 16–21% oil soluble dispersant, 14–18% iron oxide; electromagnet: steel, copper, acrylic

APPLICATIONS
Exhibits, interactive art

TYPES / SIZES
79 × 79 × 67"
(200 × 200 × 170 cm)

CONTACT
Sachiko Kodama
The University of
Electro-Communications
1-5-1 Chofugaoka,
Chofu City
Tokyo, 182-8585
Japan
Tel: +81-424-43-5537
www.kodama.hc.uec.ac.
jp/index-e.html

SOLARWALL

N° 074213-001

SOLAR AIR PANELS

The Solarwall heating and ventilation system resembles traditional metal cladding, but it also doubles as a heater. For a similar cost required to construct a metal wall, the Solarwall system provides free heating and ventilation for the life of the building.

Solarwall is an unglazed (transpired) solar collector that uses perforated sheet metal to preheat ventilation air. The system can achieve inlet air preheating of thirty to fifty degrees Fahrenheit on a sunny day, reducing the heating load on commercial and industrial buildings. Savings are dependent upon geographic location and local energy costs but range between two to eight dollars a square foot per year. Solarwall heaters also offer an optional displacement ventilation system, which spreads solar-heated fresh air over a wide area within a building.

CONTENTS
Metal

APPLICATIONS
Heating, ventilation

ENVIRONMENTAL
Lowers energy load, reduces fossil-fuel dependency, reduces carbon emissions

TESTS / EXAMINATIONS
NSTF Special Procedures—transpired collectors

CONTACT
Conserval Engineering, Inc.
220 Wildcat Road
Toronto, ON M3J 2N5
Canada
Tel: 416-661-7057
www.solarwall.com
info@solarwall.com

RECONFIGURABLE STEEL SCULPTURE

Tetra is a sculptural concept that explores the 3D extrapolation of simple growth systems in nature. It is a chain structure of multiplied modules; expressive forms and configurations may be developed from a single unit with simple rules for extrapolation. In this way, Tetra explores the idea of a very simple mechanism generating complexity in a random sequential configuration. Tetra is also hinged for flexibility and reconfigurability, so its form is never fixed.

CONTENTS
100% stainless steel

APPLICATIONS
Sculpture, space divider

TYPES / SIZES
Clear or white painted
finish

ENVIRONMENTAL
Recyclable

CONTACT
Korban Flaubert
8/8-10 Burrows Road
St. Peters, NSW 2044
Australia
Tel: +61-2-95576136
www.korbanflaubert.
com.au

INTELLIGENT PRODUCT

TICOLOR

ELECTROLYTIC METHOD FOR COLORING TITANIUM AND TITANIUM ALLOYS

Titanium and its alloys are widely used based on their chemical resistance and high mechanical performance related to relative low specific weight. While titanium has traditionally been finished in dark gray wrought or silver polished states, the material can actually exhibit a spectrum of colors when a thin, amorphous oxide layer develops on its surface.

NanoSurfaces's controlled electrochemical process allows titanium to produce unusual colors such as pink, blue, brown, green, and yellow with many different intensities and finishes. These colors are chemically resistant, may be applied to complex shapes, and are suitable for interior and exterior applications. When exposed to sunlight, the colors become particularly intense and vibrant.

CONTENTS
Titanium, titanium alloys

APPLICATIONS
Exterior and interior architectural panels, industrial products, bio-medical devices

TYPES / SIZES
31.5 × 31.5 × 16"
(80 × 80 × 40 cm)
maximum dimension

ENVIRONMENTAL
100% recyclable

CONTACT
NanoSurfaces S.R.L.
Via Matteotti 37
Cadriano di Granarolo (BO),
40057 Italy
Tel: +39 051 763824
www.nanosurfaces.it
info@nanosurfaces.it

LEAK-FREE GLAZING SYSTEM

Dr. Raymond Ting's TingWall Airloop System neutralizes the effects of both wind and rain by separating air and water seals. The result is a wall system that can tolerate imperfect seals anywhere and still not leak. In test after test, TingWall has far surpassed the most rigorous AAMA standards.

The TingWall system has also been engineered to handle seismic and wind forces, which would destroy conventional systems. In addition, various facing materials may be used without boundary problems.

CONTENTS
Aluminum, glass (or other infill materials)

APPLICATIONS
Curtain wall, window wall, sliding windows, operable windows, ribbon windows

TYPES / SIZES
Thermally broken and non-thermally broken systems

ENVIRONMENTAL
Watertight system prevents poor indoor air quality related to mold growth

TESTS / EXAMINATIONS
ASTM E283, ASTM E330, ASTM E331

CONTACT
TingWall Inc.
505A McKnight Park Drive
Pittsburgh, PA 15237
Tel: 412-367-2808
www.tingwall.com
4info@tingwall.com

INTELLIGENT PRODUCT

THERMALLY EFFICIENT STEEL FRAMING SYSTEM

ULTRAPERFORMING PRODUCT

A recycled steel stud system can be an environmentally superior choice to virgin wood studs, but thermal bridging between the highly conductive steel studs and the building envelope presents a challenge for energy-efficient design.

Tri-Chord Steel Systems manufacturers the most thermally efficient steel framing components available. Tri-Chord studs have the highest thermal, seismic, acoustic, and fire ratings for steel framing and will meet the thermal transference of wood. Tri-Chord Steel Studs are structural and will carry up to 5,170 pounds per stud. They are also one-hour fire rated on load bearing interior and exterior walls.

The Tri-Chord Stud and Truss Systems were designed to minimize thermal bridging, and contain sixty-six to sixty-eight percent postconsumer recycled content from wrecked automobiles and other sources. In profile, the studs and trusses have triangular sections at each edge and discreet webs spanning the wall cavity, instead of a solid heat-conducting steel webs. Tri-Chord Steel also offers floor trusses (CRS), which span great distances due to the strength of the triangular profile.

CONTENTS
Postconsumer recycled steel (up to 66%)

APPLICATIONS
Structural and non-structural framing

TYPES / SIZES
3.5" (8.9 cm) and 5.5" (14 cm) studs, purlin and track, 1.1, 1.3, and 1.7" (2.7, 3.3, and 4.3 cm)

ENVIRONMENTAL
Recycled content, energy efficiency

TESTS / EXAMINATIONS
ICC accepted, ERS 1158, STC and OITC rated on various wall configurations, racking shear tested, wind load tested, thermally tested

CONTACT
Tri-Chord Steel Systems, Inc.
3639 East Superior
Phoenix, AZ 85040
Tel: 512-415-2878
www.tri-chordsteel.com

VIARO

INTELLIGENT INFRASTRUCTURE FOR POWER, DATA, AND DISPLAY SYSTEMS

Designed by Danny Hillis, Bran Ferren, and Sheila Kennedy, Viaro is intended to catalyze a new generation of radically flexible interior spaces. By combining its open, modular building power infrastructure with an array of space-making elements and manufacturing capabilities, Viaro enables the creation of environments that are rapidly and inexpensively reconfigurable. Powered by Viaro, new or renovated interior spaces become programmable environments, responsive to the ever-changing ways in which people work, play, shop, heal, and live.

Manufactured by Herman Miller, Viaro consists of a system of ceiling-mounted rails that hosts a modular power distribution system and a communication and control system. The combination of power, data, and structural support for communications and display equipment enables the occupants of a space to program peer-to-peer connections between plugged-in devices. The Viaro infrastructure is modular, so that occupants or facility owners can upgrade interior spaces on an as-needed basis. Viaro is also mobile and reusable: it can be entirely disassembled from its original site and reinstalled in other locations.

CONTENTS
Steel, ABS, aluminum

APPLICATIONS
Infrastructure for lighting, digital displays, screens, projectors, curtains, partitions, and other fixtures

TYPES / SIZES
5' (1.5 m) and 10' (3 m) steel rails, modular plug assemblies

ENVIRONMENTAL
Recyclable

TESTS / EXAMINATIONS
UL listed

LIMITATIONS
Not for exterior use

CONTACT
Herman Miller, Inc.
855 East Main Avenue
Zeeland, MI 49464
Tel: 616-654-8257
www.hermanmiller.
com/viaro
viaro@hermanmiller.com

ZINC FOAM

ZINC-FOAM PLATES, SANDWICHES, AND 3D PARTS

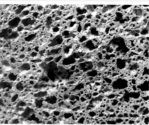

Developed by the Fraunhofer Institute for Machine Tools and Forming Technology, Zinc Foam is a low density, low weight, and resilient manifestation of zinc. These properties make it a great material to be used in fast-moving components and/or components demanding absorption. The zinc foam can be either glued to another material or become a metallic compound with the material.

A zinc-foam sandwich, consisting of two cover sheets and a layer of zinc foam in the middle, greatly expands the field of application. The cover sheets greatly contribute stiffness, while the foam contributes cushioning. The sandwiches can be welded together just like normal sheet metal.

CONTENTS
Zinc and zinc alloys

APPLICATIONS
Cushioning, thermal isolation, shock absorption

TYPES / SIZES
59 × 55" (150 × 140 cm) maximum plate size, 3D shapes

ENVIRONMENTAL
High strength-to-weight ratio

LIMITATIONS
Thermally unstable above 392° F (200° C)

CONTACT
Fraunhofer Institute
Reichenhainer Straße 88
Chemnitz, 09126
Germany
Tel: +0049-371-5397-456
www.iwu.fhg.de/
schaumzentrum/english

04: **WOOD**

3D VENEER

3D FORMABLE WOOD VENEER

3D Veneer is a formable veneer for the industrial production of 3D molded plywood developed by Dr. Achim Moeller. The 3D Veneer process first treats conventional wood veneers in such a way that they can be "deep drawn," while preserving the texture of the wood.

In this way, it is possible to create plywood products that were impossible to make before. The 3D shells can also be laminated, making use of the well-known advantages of lightweight construction and 3D sandwich structures.

Apart from the manufacture of molded parts, 3D veneers can be also used for coating 3D components like housings in a wide range of materials.

CONTENTS
100% wood

APPLICATIONS
Furniture, products, automobile industry parts

TYPES / SIZES
Beech, oak, maple, walnut, and other wood types; custom sizes. Maximum size: 79" (200 cm) length, 38.5" (98 cm) width

ENVIRONMENTAL
Less material required due to high stiffness of 3D form

TESTS / EXAMINATIONS
EN 1728, DIN V ENV 12520

LIMITATIONS
Not for exterior use

CONTACT
Reholz GmbH
Sachsenallee 11,
Kesselsdorf, 01723
Germany
Tel: +49-35204 78 04 30
www.reholz.de
info@reholz.de

SOLID HARDWOOD THAT CAN BE BENT IN A COLD, DRY STATE

Bendywood is solid hardwood that can easily be bent while cold and dry to a radius of ten times its thickness. Thin sections can be bent by hand and thicker sections with the application of sufficient force. Handrails can be bent into shape, table edges can be profiled and then bent and glued into place, and sculptural forms can be created quickly and with ease. Bendywood can be worked like normal wood and can offer great time savings, cost savings, and a better finished product compared to traditional wood bending or laminating techniques.

ULTRAPERFORMING MATERIAL

CONTENTS
100% wood (European beech, oak, maple, or ash)

APPLICATIONS
Handrails, round tabletop edges, circular wall rails, furniture, sculpture

TYPES / SIZES
3 × 4 × 65" (8 × 10 × 165 cm) maximum size

ENVIRONMENTAL
No chemicals used in manufacture

LIMITATIONS
Not for exterior use

CONTACT
Candidus Prugger Sas
Via Johann Kravogl 10
Bressanone, 39042
Italy
Tel: +390472834530
www.bendywood.com

BL SPECIAL

LAMINATED WOOD COMPOSITE PANELS FOR USE WITH LASER CUTTER

Designed by Steven Holl with Nick Gelpi, Alberto Martinuzzo, and Alessandro Orsini, BL Special is a composite panel comprised of wood veneers and a proprietary substrate. BL Special was developed to overcome limitations presented by conventional composite panels when modified with a laser cutter.

BL stands for "Bi-Legno," which translates as two layers of wood. The material may be readily folded along scored lines and is designed for the assembly of complex geometric structures as well as rapid prototyping applications.

CONTENTS
50% wood veneer, 50% proprietary core materials

APPLICATIONS
Paneling for assembly of complex, self-supported volumetric geometries

TYPES / SIZES
120 × 45" (305 × 115 cm) maximum dimensions

ENVIRONMENTAL
Optimized use of material

LIMITATIONS
Not yet for exterior use

CONTACT
Ableflex
1/a, Str. Delle Paludi-Francenigo
di Gaiarine (Tv), 31010
Italy
Tel: +39-0434-768492
www.albeflex.it
info@albeflex.it

CRISTAL DE RAVIER

LAMINATED WOOD AND ACRYLIC BLOCKS

Cristal de Ravier highlights the combination between wood and acrylic in order to obtain luxury and decorative effects for use in furniture and interior design. The material is manufactured in either panels or blocks of different sizes and thicknesses according to the design requirements. Different woods are used based on the desired color, and the acrylic is available in glossy or frosted finishes.

CONTENTS
Wood and acrylic in different proportions

APPLICATIONS
Cabinetry, tabletops, desktops, partition walls, furniture, hand railings, stairs, decoration items

TYPES / SIZES
Custom

LIMITATIONS
Not for exterior use

CONTACT
Ravier SA
Chemin Vergerot
Domblans, 39210
France
Tel: +33 3 84 44 61 08
www.ravier.fr
info@ravier.fr

DURAPALM

PALM FLOORING AND PLYWOOD

Smith & Fong works with a coconut palm found abundantly in Asia. Plantation-grown palms produce nuts for more than a hundred years, but as palms get taller with age, nutrients traveling from the base cannot reach the nuts efficiently, thus diminishing production. The taller palms are eventually removed and replaced with younger, better producers. The felled timber, which is a by-product of the palm plantation, has no established secondary market and frequently goes unused.

Smith & Fong is developing this secondary market to provide a greater cash return to the farmer and a greater utilization of this valuable material. As the rain forests of these regions continue to be tapped for timber needs, coconut palm lumber has been an overlooked resource. According to the manufacturer, "We hope through this work [that] palm will one day be recognized as a valuable building alternative and help reduce rain forest harvesting."

CONTENTS
Coconut palm lumber

APPLICATIONS
Flooring, paneling, cabinetry

TYPES / SIZES
Flooring: 3/4" × 3" × 2–6' (1.9 cm × 7.5 cm × .6–1.8 m), prefinished or unfinished plywood: 3/4 × 30 × 72" (1.9 × 76 × 183 cm)

ENVIRONMENTAL
Reclaimed lumber

TESTS / EXAMINATIONS
ASTM E648, D1037, D1037-99, D4060, D2394

LIMITATIONS
Not for exterior use

CONTACT
Smith & Fong
375 Oyster Point Blvd, #3
San Francisco, CA 94080
Tel: 866-835-9859
www.durapalm.com
info@durapalm.com

LIGHTWEIGHT WHEAT STRAW AND PAPER CONSTRUCTION SYSTEM

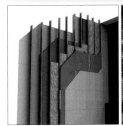

ULTRAPERFORMING PRODUCT

Durra Building Systems manufactures engineered acoustic wall, roof, and ceiling systems for venues such as theaters, airports, convention centers, and other spaces that have high acoustic demands.

The Durra Acoustic Panel is made from wheat straw and recycled paper, and it eliminates the need for multiple layers of drywall and up to half the studs used with conventional systems based on its structural rigidity.

The Durra Roofing System combines the roof with the finished ceiling, allowing both economic and construction-time savings. The Durra roof is constructed on the ground in sections of one thousand square feet and flown into place. In this way, each section can be installed at a rate of every two hours.

CONTENTS
Compressed wheat straw, recycled paper, roll-formed steel

APPLICATIONS
Theaters, convention centers, arenas, performing arts centers, airports, distribution centers, mixed-use projects, manufacturing facilities, and any space with stringent noise-transmission requirements

TYPES / SIZES
Standard panel size: 4' × 8' × 2" (1.2 m × 2.4 m × 5 cm); custom sizes available

ENVIRONMENTAL
Use of agricultural by-product and recycled materials; no added chemicals; efficient use of material

TESTS / EXAMINATIONS
UL rated; sound, fire, and ASTM test data available upon request

CONTACT
Durra Building Systems
2747 State Highway 160
Whitewright, TX 75491
Tel: 866-364-1198
www.durra.com
sales@durra.com

EGGSHELL

LACQUERED EGGSHELL-SURFACED WOOD PANELS

 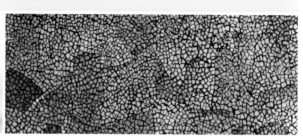

Made entirely by hand in Vietnam, these panels are a product of a long history of decorative inlay technique indigenous to Vietnam. Duck eggs are roasted over a grill, crushed, and placed into a chestnut lacquer matrix on a marine plywood substrate. This composite is then rubbed by hand into a smooth polished finish under running water. This process takes fifty days to complete from start to finish. Abalone shells are also available in the same chestnut lacquer matrix.

Colors include deep red, blue, and red dot. Applications include vertical and horizontal surfacing. Custom sizes, colors, and patterns are available.

CONTENTS
Plywood, duck eggshell, or abalone shell, lacquer

APPLICATIONS
Vertical and horizontal interior surfacing

TYPES / SIZES
4' × 8' × 3/4" (1.2 m × 2.4 m × 2 cm), 5 colors

LIMITATIONS
Not for exterior use

CONTACT
Robin Reigi Inc.
48 West 21st Street
New York, NY 10010
Tel: 212-924-5558
www.robin-reigi.com
info@robin-reigi.com

LIGHTWEIGHT COMPOSITE FOLDING BOARD

Timm Herok developed Foldtex as a lightweight folding material in order to challenge traditional notions of product fittings, corner connections and surface finishing techniques. Foldtex consists of at least two layers, one is flexible, the other is stiff. When incisions are made in the stiff layer, thus exposing the flexible layer below, a folding hinge is created.

Folding grooves may be made via CNC milling, although simple folds may be made with a handheld milling machine. Separation cuts are then completed using a cutting knife. Foldtex can be individually adapted in its strength and surface qualities through the use of veneers, layering, staining, and painting. A high finish may be achieved either before or after the milling of the template.

CONTENTS
60–80% wallboard, 15–30% recycled leather, 5–10% silicone

APPLICATIONS
Furniture design, model-building, lightweight load-bearing structures, and textile design; designed for the application of CNC techniques

TYPES / SIZES
Combination of wallboard (.1 or .05", .3 or .1 cm) and one or two-sided coating (.02", .05 cm); 55 × 83" (140 × 210 cm) panels, 1300g/m–2200g/m

ENVIRONMENTAL
Utilizes renewable and recyclable materials efficiently

LIMITATIONS
Not for exterior use

CONTACT
Timm Herok
Georg-Treser-Str. 49
Frankfurt, AM D-60599
Germany
Tel: +49 (0) 69-71034393
www.foldtex.com
info@foldtex.com

GOUGED COLLECTION

MILLED INTEGRAL-COLOR MDF AND WOOD VENEER PANELS

Architectural Systems offers a collection of wood and integral-color MDF panels with a striking 3D-milled surface effect. A variety of milling surface patterns, wood veneers, and specialty finishes, such as matte velour, stains, and pearlescent colors, are available. The panels may be hung, affixed, or incorporated into any interior flat or curved surface. Panel thickness varies according to the selected substrate material.

CONTENTS
MDF and wood veneers

APPLICATIONS
Feature walls, reception areas, ceilings, bar fronts, doors, screens, architectural millwork, store fixturing, furniture

TYPES / SIZES
Gouged MDF and wood veneer: 48 × 118" (122 × 300 cm); through-color MDF: 72 × 98" (183 × 249 cm)

LIMITATIONS
For interior use only

CONTACT
Architectural Systems, Inc.
150 West 25th Street
8th Floor
New York, NY 10001
Tel: 800-793-0224
www.archsystems.com
sales@archsystems.com

IN-OUT CURTAIN

CONFIGURABLE WOOD-VENEER CURTAIN

In-Out Curtain is a prototype design for an operable screen that can be manipulated to change shape in section as well as in plan. Made from thin wood veneer or paper, it is conceived as a hybrid drape/ Venetian blind that may function either as a window covering or a transformable room partition.

The curtain is comprised of cut, perforated, folded, and interlocked laser-cut modules. The modules are each designed with internal tensions so that they hold two distinct shapes, a closed/concave shape, and an open/convex one. The modules, when linked together, translate their individual deformation onto adjacent areas, creating a curtain of multiple shape variation. The overall pattern is algorithmically derived, based on room location and/or light direction.

Each curtain can have a unique form and can be altered continuously by hand. In-Out Curtain explores relationships between the specificity and precision of digital fabrication and the ability of the user to alter the end product at will.

CONTENTS
Wood veneer, internal mylar structure, zinc eyelets

APPLICATIONS
Window treatment, interior partition, room enclosure

TYPES / SIZES
Customizable dimensions

ENVIRONMENTAL
Made with rapidly renewable wood veneer that emits no VOCs and uses very little raw material

LIMITATIONS
Not for exterior use

CONTACT
IwamotoScott
777 Florida Street
Suite 308
San Francisco, CA 94110
Tel: 415-643-7773
www.iwamotoscott.com

KIREI BOARD

SORGHUM-BASED ARCHITECTURAL MILLWORK MATERIAL

Kirei Board is a finish material with a dramatic grain and eco-friendly properties used for paneling, cabinetry, casework, furniture, retail displays, tabletops, and flooring. Comprised of the reclaimed stalks of sorghum grown around the world for food, the working properties of Kirei Board are similar to plywood, and it may be nailed, screwed, glued, and finished with standard wood-finishing techniques.

CONTENTS
85% sorghum straw,
10% KR bond adhesive,
5% poplar

APPLICATIONS
Decorative paneling, mill-work, cabinetry, furniture, ceilings, flooring

TYPES / SIZES
3 × 6' (.9 × 1.8 m) sheets in .4, .8, and 1.2" (1, 2, and 3 cm) thicknesses

ENVIRONMENTAL
Postindustrial recycled material, rapidly renewable resource, zero VOC emissions

LIMITATIONS
Not for exterior use or high-traffic flooring applications

CONTACT
Kirei USA
640 10th Avenue
San Diego, CA 92101
Tel: 619-236-9924
www.kireiusa.com

LUMINATE

FUSED WOOD AND TRANSLUCENT ACRYLIC

Luminate combines translucent plastic and wood strips in a rigid panel format, allowing light to filter through a material used for applications that would usually require an opaque surface. The material is a modified acrylic adhered to selected exotic timbers with a proprietary fusion process. The manufacturer has also recently combined colored finishes with the translucent strips.

CONTENTS

90% wood-based products, 10% modified acrylic resin

APPLICATIONS

Doors, screens, partitions, ceiling panels, feature floor panels, stairs, counters, table tops, bench tops, furniture

TYPES / SIZES

Strips .16, .35, or 1" (.4, .9, or 2.5 cm) wide; panels vary in thickness from .4 to 1.6" (1 to 4 cm)

ENVIRONMENTAL

Uses 25% as much hardwood as conventional solid wood panels

LIMITATIONS

Conditional exterior use

CONTACT

Ambro Australia Pty. Ltd.
PO Box 237
Virginia, 5120
Australia
Tel: +61 08 8380 9544
www.ambro.com.au
create@ambro.com.au

NOVACORK

CORK VENEER OVER RECYCLED-PAPER SUBSTRATE

NovaCork panels are ideal for tackable surface applications located in high-traffic areas. The combination of post-consumer recycled cork and a post-consumer recycled Homasote substrate provides a durable and environmentally sustainable alternative to conventional cork boards. NovaCork panels are also available with a Class A fire-rating.

CONTENTS
Recycled cork, recycled paper

APPLICATIONS
Tackboard, finished wall covering, space dividers

TYPES / SIZES
2 × 3' (.6 × .9 m), 3 × 4' (.9 × 1.2 m), and 4 × 8' (1.2 × 2.4 m) panels; 1/2" (1.3 cm) thick

ENVIRONMENTAL
High recycled content, low embodied energy

TESTS / EXAMINATIONS
440 Homasote substrate: UL listing R16381, ASTM E-84 Flame Spread Class C

NCFR Homasote substrate: UL listings R5268, 91G7; ASTM E-84 Flame Spread Class A

LIMITATIONS
Not recommended for flooring underlayment or exterior exposure

CONTACT
Homasote
932 Lower Ferry Road
West Trenton, NJ 08628
Tel: 800-257-9491
www.homasote.com
sales@homasote.com

PLY

UNDULATING PLYWOOD SURFACE

  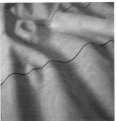 

Ply is a sculptural-wall element made of birch wood harvested in Finland. The textile-thin birch plywood layer is nearly translucent (at 0.45 mm). This layer is adhered to a solid birch frame, which may be mounted to straight surfaces using a variety of methods.

Ply is available in two versions, the curvilinear Ply1 and the gentle wave profile Ply2. Mirror image tiles are also available to allow for continuous wave patterns. Ply may be assembled horizontally or vertically, and may be backlit for a dramatic effect. The standard surface is lacquered natural birch, but Ply may also be stained dark gray or natural white.

CONTENTS
50% birch plywood, 50% solid birch

APPLICATIONS
Feature walls, acoustic paneling, sculpture

TYPES / SIZES
23.5 × 23.5"
(59.5 × 59.5 cm)

ENVIRONMENTAL
Recyclable

TESTS / EXAMINATIONS
ISO acoustic tests

LIMITATIONS
Not for exterior use

CONTACT
Showroom Finland Oy
Puistokatu 7A
Helsinki, FIN-00140
Finland
Tel: +358-9-6811 940
www.showroomfinland.fi
info@showroomfinland.fi

STRANDWOVEN BAMBOO

COMPRESSED AND DENSIFIED BAMBOO HARDWOOD FLOORING

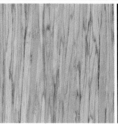

Strandwoven bamboo is one of the most durable hardwoods known. Used typically for hardwood flooring (and other millwork components), Strandwoven bamboo is suitable both in residential and high-traffic commercial applications. Thin filaments of bamboo are mixed in a low-VOC heat sensitive resin and compressed under intense pressures to form a consistent and extremely dense log/beam. This log is then milled into the required dimension.

Strandwoven bamboo is not only superior in its hardness and stability, it is also superior in its environmental attributes. Bamboo is a grass and grows up to sixty feet in height in a couple of months, at which time it is left to internally mature before harvesting. Unmatched with any other wood used in construction, Strandwoven bamboo uses eighty-four percent of the raw material harvested (for comparison, "traditional" bamboo flooring, which uses material significantly more effectively than any other wood, uses only sixty-five percent of the raw material harvested) in addition to using a significant percentage of postindustrial scrap, which would otherwise be burned.

CONTENTS
Bamboo fibers, low-VOC resin

APPLICATIONS
Hardwood flooring, structural beams and columns, architectural millwork

TYPES / SIZES
Flooring planks, panels, shelving units

ENVIRONMENTAL
Rapidly renewable, made from postindustrial scraps, low VOCs

TESTS / EXAMINATIONS
ASTM standard tests for hardwoods

LIMITATIONS
Not yet for exterior use

CONTACT
Strandwoven Wood Company
PO Box 1831
Boulder, CO 80306
Tel: 720-564-4922
www.strandwoven.com
info@strandwoven.com

ELECTRIFIED PREFORMED WOOD

Wood.e is essentially electrified wood. Furniture made of Wood.e, with an electrical current of twelve volts, permits one to easily plug in different applications (plug and play). Wood.e is a built-up composite comprised of plywood and two integrated conducting layers. These layers allow for unprecedented possibilities for sound, light, and motion to be combined seamlessly with wood furniture.

Designed by Bjorn Blisse, Folker Konigbauer, and Reinhard Zetsche from Transalpin, the project "Living in a Box" is a furniture system made out of Wood.e, and demonstrates the potential of this material. Stand-alone furniture like chairs, tables, lamps, and shelves create symbiotic relationships that are not possible with ordinary wood or metal, and previously isolated objects can now combine the functions of furniture, lighting, and space definition.

CONTENTS
Wood, aluminum

APPLICATIONS
Furniture

LIMITATIONS
Only for currents up
to 24 V

CONTACT
Becker KG
PO Box 1164
Brakel, D-33026
Germany
Tel: +49 (0) 8261 6941
www.transalpin.net

RECOMBINANT PRODUCT

05: **PLASTIC + RUBBER**

ALGUES

POLYPROPYLENE BIOMIMETIC MODULES

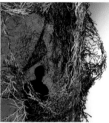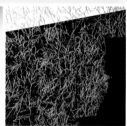

Ronan & Erwan Bouroullec's Algues (French for "algae") is a biomimetic sculptural system based on a multibranched plastic module that can be attached to other modules with plastic pegs through its nineteen ringlets. Algues may be used to create flexible room partitions, curtains, sculpture, etc.

CONTENTS
Injected polypropylene

APPLICATIONS
Flexible partitions, sculpture

TYPES / SIZES
10.5 × 9 × 1.5"
(27 × 23 × 4 cm)

CONTACT
Vitra GmbH
Charles-Eames-Strasse 2
Weil am Rhein, 79576
Germany
Tel: +49 00 800 22 55 84 87
www.vitra.com
info@vitra.com

BELLA RIFATTA

RECYCLED-PET STACKABLE CHAIR

Designed by William Sawaya, Bella Rifatta is a stackable chair made of recycled PET. It is available in white, gray, and black with a matte finish. The chair is appropriate for outdoor as well as indoor use and is stackable up to twenty pieces. The Bella Rifatta is also available in semitransparent polycarbonate and white propylene versions.

CONTENTS
77% recycled PET, 23% reinforced glass fiber, and elastomers

APPLICATIONS
Chair suitable for interior and exterior use

TYPES / SIZES
2.3 × 2.1 × 3.2"
(5.85 × 5.4 × 8.1 cm)

ENVIRONMENTAL
Recycled material

CONTACT
Sawaya & Moroni
Via Andegari 18
Milan, 20121
Italy
Tel: +0039-02-86-395-221
www.sawayamoroni.com
info@sawayamoroni.com

BODYPROPS

POLYURETHANE MORPHOLOGICAL CUSHIONS

Bodyprops are five soft forms molded in expanded polyurethane with elastic varnish finish, created as an extension of the body for support in all its different postures. "I thought of living in a house as a physical exercise," relates creator Olivier Peyricot. "In sport the body offers an increasingly unbelievable performance. Body props are an invitation to conquer space as in a sport competition."

Body props are supports for lying on the ground, propped on one elbow or in a comfortable kneeling position, to use in bed like a work surface, or to kneel in order to relieve the pressure of the spine.

Four have ergonomic forms whose symmetry derives from that of the body. The fifth item is asymmetrical and invites a more personal use. The project was developed in collaboration with VIA (Valorization of Furnishing Innovation) in Paris and introduces a new philosophy of comfort that embraces the floor as a living space.

CONTENTS
100% polyurethane

APPLICATIONS
Floor seating

TYPES / SIZES
19.5 × 17.5" (50 × 45 cm)

CONTACT
Edra SPA
PO Box 28
Perignano (PI), Italy
Tel: +39 05876 16660
www.edra.com
edra@edra.com

CAST RESIN

CAST POLYURETHANE AND POLYESTER RESIN

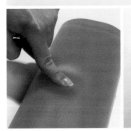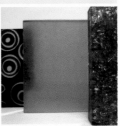

Brookyln-based Charles Hickok has developed techniques for casting polyurethane and polyester-based resins in a wide array of colors, hardnesses, and finishes.

Polyurethane may be cast in hard, rubber, or gel formats, and these qualities may be combined in layers for abrasion-resistance. Polyurethane resin is water-clear and UV resistant and is recommended for both interior and exterior applications. Polyurethane cast resin must be supported every 18 inches, with a maximum overhang of 9 inches.

Polyester resin is less expensive than polyurethane and is not UV resistant or perfectly water-clear. Polyester resin is available only as a hard, smooth surface with a satin or glossy finish. It is more brittle than polyurethane and is especially susceptible to thermal expansion and contraction. It must be supported every 12 inches, with a maximum overhang of 6 inches. Polyester resin is not fire rated and is only recommended for interior applications.

CONTENTS
100% polyurethane or 100% polyester

APPLICATIONS
Horizontal surfacing: bar tops, tabletops, countertops with integral sinks; vertical surfacing: doors, wall panels, partition panels

TYPES / SIZES
Standard slab size up to 5 × 10' (1.5 × 3 m)

ENVIRONMENTAL
Cast polyurethane is inert after curing and will not off-gas

LIMITATIONS
In horizontal applications, polyurethane must be supported every 18" (45.5 cm) and polyester must be supported every 12" (30.5 cm) to prevent sagging

CONTACT
Robin Reigi Inc. with Charles Hickok Industrial Design
48 West 21st Street
New York, NY 10010
Tel: 212-924-5558
www.robin-reigi.com
info@robin-reigi.com

CD

RECYCLED COMPACT DISCS

Confiscated illicit CDs are crushed and dispersed within a pale blue, transparent polycarbonate matrix that is comprised of recycled cold-water drink containers.

CONTENTS
Recycled compact discs, recycled polycarbonate

APPLICATIONS
Work surfaces, furniture, backsplashes, shower surrounds

TYPES / SIZES
47 × 31.5 × .5" (120 × 80 × 1.2 cm) thick panels

ENVIRONMENTAL
100% recycled content

CONTACT
Smile Plastics Ltd.
Mansion House, Ford
Shrewsbury, SY5 9LZ UK
Tel: +01743 850267
www.smile-plastics.co.uk
smileplas@aol.com

CLOUD MODULE

POLYSTYRENE SHELVING SYSTEM

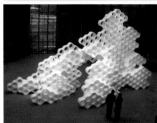 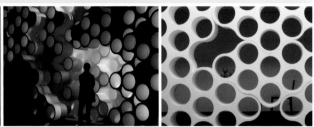

Ronan & Erwan Bouroullec's Cloud Modules are modular shelving units made of white polystyrene. The Cloud system was conceived as the proliferation of a shared abstract form, like a growing plant, stubbornly repeating its structure of nodes. These nodes are designed to grow within architectural spaces with a kind of biological intelligence that is inherent in the system.

INTELLIGENT PRODUCT

CONTENTS
100% polystyrene

APPLICATIONS
Shelving, space divider

TYPES / SIZES
41 × 74 × 16"
(105 × 187.5 × 40 cm)

CONTACT
Cap Design SPA
Via Marconi 35
Arosio, 22060 Italy
Tel: +39 031 759111
www.cappellini.it
cappellini@cappellini.it

CUBIX

FURNITURE VENDING MACHINE

Developed by Transalpin, Cubix is a vending machine that generates instant furniture from 3D textiles and various composite materials. Whether a chair, table, shelf, or light, each piece is prepared and delivered in a cube measuring 6.3 × 6.3 × 6.3" (16 × 16 × 16 cm). The furniture automatically unfolds and inflates to its desired form when the user pulls a red line supplied with the cube.

Cubix was developed for the Milan Salone Satellite in 2003 by Bjorn Blisse, Folker Koenigbauer, and Reinhard Zetsche of Transalpin.

CONTENTS
3D textiles and composite materials

APPLICATIONS
Furniture industries

ENVIRONMENTAL
Efficient use of materials

CONTACT
Transalpin
Troppauer Strasse 15
Mindelheim, D-87719
Germany
Tel: +49 0 8261 6941
www.transalpin.net

DAPPLE

RECYCLED POLYETHYLENE SHEET

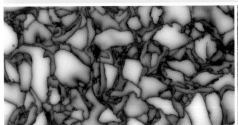 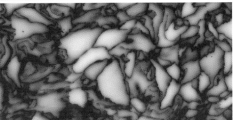

Dapple is made from shredded industrial foodstuff containers mixed with some factory scrap. Colored veins are added in the recycling process. Standard colors are black, red, or blue, and custom colors are also available.

CONTENTS

100% recycled high molecular weight polyethylene

APPLICATIONS

Work surfaces, furniture, backsplashes, shower surrounds

TYPES / SIZES

79 × 39.5" (200 × 100 cm) panels up to 1" (2.5 cm) thick

ENVIRONMENTAL

100% recycled content

CONTACT

Smile Plastics Ltd.
Mansion House, Ford
Shrewsbury, SY5 9LZ UK
Tel: +01743 850267
www.smile-plastics.co.uk
smileplas@aol.com

EVA COLLECTION

ETHYLENE VINYL ACETATE PRODUCTS

   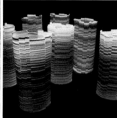

EVA is a common hot-melt adhesive or hot glue. Tony Wurman has developed several proprietary techniques for working with this material to give it the reflective and refractive qualities of glass, but with the modulation of rubber and longevity of plastic.

In its explorations, Wunderwurks Design has been able to create objects using traditional techniques found in glass or ceramics design that would normally be cost prohibitive in those materials. The EVA Collection represents the fulfillment of a mission to transform a common industrial product into a new art and design medium.

CONTENTS
100% ethylene vinyl acetate

APPLICATIONS
Furniture, lighting, bowls, trays, vases, clocks, jewelry, clothing

ENVIRONMENTAL
100% recyclable, nontoxic, all excess material is reconstituted to be used in new products or product parts

LIMITATIONS
Not for use in extreme hot or freezing cold environments

CONTACT
Wunderwurks Design
160 Sixth Avenue, Suite #1
New York, NY 10013
Tel: 212-431-6625
www.wunderwurks.com

FLEXIBLE POLYPROPYLENE HONEYCOMB PANELS

REPURPOSED MATERIAL

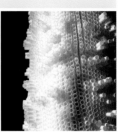

Imagine a mix between a beehive and a slinky: Flexicomb is a light-hearted new material that combines the properties of both. In contrast to conventional rigid honeycombs, Flexicomb is flexible, bouncy, and fun. This porous, translucent material transmits light effectively, and it can be bent, sprung, and compressed to form sculptural installations, lamps, desktop accessories, and furniture prototypes.

PadLAb makes Flexicomb by fusing thousands of closely packed polypropylene tubes on one end to form a flexible honeycomb. The production of Flexicomb begins with a set of tightly compressed cylinders. When the ends of the closely packed tubes are heated, they fuse into a matrix of hexagons.

The idea for Flexicomb grew out of PadLAb co-founder Dan Gottlieb's research project on structural honeycomb at the Yale School of Architecture. Commercial aerospace and transportation-grade honeycombs exceeded a student budget, so Gottlieb decided to make his own, out of a more economical raw material: drinking straws. Dan's experiments making furniture out of straws included the use of slim red coffee-stirrers and fat fluorescent super-straws.

CONTENTS

100% polypropylene tubes

APPLICATIONS

Lighting, interior room dividers, ceiling panels, sculptural installations, functional objects

TYPES / SIZES

14 × 22 × 1/2" or 3" (35.5 × 56 × 1.3 or 7.5 cm) thick, in white, with 1/4" (.6 cm) diameter tubes; custom colors, tube diameters and panel sizes available

ENVIRONMENTAL

Readaptation and reevaluation of plastic drinking straws, a disposable everyday product

LIMITATIONS

Not recommended for exterior use; compact fluorescent bulbs or other low heat bulbs are recommend for lighting applications

CONTACT

PadLAb
612 Moulton Avenue, #1
Los Angeles, CA 90031
Tel: 323-441-9189
www.padlab.com
pad@padlab.com

FLEXISURF

RECYCLED PVC FLOORING

Swimming pool covers, industrial roofing membranes, and tons of automobile upholstery trim scrap are landfilled every year. These materials are made of PVC plastic with polyester strands added to increase overall product rigidity and physical strength. Commingled plastics such as these are practically impossible to separate for recycling, but combined as Flexisurf they each play an important part in the material's quality and durability.

Originally conceived as recycled resilient industrial flooring, Flexisurf is also finding its way into a variety of other applications. Flexisurf can be cut with a knife, saw, router, die, water-jet, and laser. It can be applied bonded or unbonded to any flat, clean, hard, and dry surface. Seams can be welded chemically or by heat to produce watertight joints.

Flexisurf will not shrink, buckle, warp or crack, and it is easy to clean and maintain. It is stain, chemical, weather, impact, corrosion, and puncture resistant. Flexisurf is treated with Vinyzene fungicide to resist mold and bacterial growth. The nonskid, resilient surface reduces noise, and it is a completely safe, nontoxic material that causes no harm to the environment during its manufacture or use. Flexisurf is also available with a factory-applied UV-cured urethane finish.

CONTENTS
Recycled PVC and polyester

APPLICATIONS
Resilient flooring, tabletop surfaces, self-healing cutting surfaces, ladder treads, mouse pads

TYPES / SIZES
18 × 18" (45.5 × 45.5 cm),
24 × 24" (61 × 61 cm),
60 × 60" (152.5 × 152.5 cm),
60 × 96" (152.5 × 244 cm)
sheets

ENVIRONMENTAL
Recycled content, low VOCs

CONTACT
Yemm & Hart Ltd.
(via Robin Reigi Inc.)
48 West 21st Street
New York, NY 10010
Tel: 212-924-5558
www.robin-reigi.com
info@robin-reigi.com

3D VOLUMETRIC POLYURETHANE ELEMENT FOR INTERIORS

INTELLIGENT MATERIAL

OMA developed Foam as part of their work for Prada. In addition to the design of new spatial typologies, the development of new materials expands the interior palette of the new Prada epicenter stores. Ranging from translucent cast resin for shelves to bubble-textured silicone floor mats, the creation of this new substance manifests a radical redefinition of surface and material.

Foam is a polyurethane cast of an aggregate condition between solid and void. It is both a regular and irregular structure of spongelike consistency that can be cast in stages from hard to soft, and from transparent to opaque. It forms a substance that can be used to build objects as well as entire spaces, a further interpretation of solid and void.

Foam was developed beginning with an architectural model using a regular cleaning sponge. Because the visual effect of this backlit texture was very intriguing, OMA initiated an extensive search to recreate this material in 1:1 scale. The architect made hundreds of prototypes in order to test hole sizes, percentages of openness, translucencies, depths, colors, etc.

In its multiple and varied manifestations, Foam offers a new definition of functional and visual properties between artificial and natural, irregular and regular, transparent and opaque, translucent and solid, flexible and rigid qualities in the design of interior environments.

CONTENTS
100% polyurethane

APPLICATIONS
Interior finish, furniture, light object

TYPES / SIZES
4'-6" × 9' × 4" (1.4 m × 2.7 m × 10 cm)

LIMITATIONS
Developed exclusively for Prada

CONTACT
Office for Metropolitan Architecture
Heer Bokelweg 149
Rotterdam, 3032 AD
The Netherlands
Tel: +31-10-243 8200
www.oma.nl
office@oma.nl

GRASSPAVE2

GRASS POROUS PAVING SYSTEM

Grasspave2 is a recycled plastic porous paving system designed to add green space and environmental benefits while providing a paved surface. The Grasspave2 system is comprised of a sandy gravel base course, a Hydrogrow polymer-fertilizer mixture, the Grasspave2 ring-and-grid structure, sharp concrete sand, and grass seed or sod.

Grasspave2 provides incredible load-bearing strength, while protecting vegetation root systems from compaction. High void spaces within the entire cross-section enable excellent root development and storage capacity for rainfall from storm events. Stormwater is slowed through Grasspave2 surfaces, which deposits suspended sediment and increases discharge time. Suspended pollutants and moderate amounts of engine oils are consumed by active soil bacteria, which are aided by the system's excellent oxygen exchange capacity.

CONTENTS

100% recycled HDPE plastic, hydrogrow (polymer/fertilizer)

APPLICATIONS

Turf reinforcement for parking lots, fire lanes, emergency access drives, driveways, trails, golf cart paths, infiltration basins, swale reinforcement, pedestrian access

ENVIRONMENTAL

100% recycled plastic, urban heat island mitigation, stormwater runoff mitigation, hydrocarbon and other pollutant filtering, groundwater recharge, airborne dust capture and retention, air-conditioning effect

TESTS / EXAMINATIONS

Compression tests

LIMITATIONS

Low speed (vehicle) and low frequency travel: 2 days on, 1 day off (or 5 days on with 1 day off), maximum speed 25 mph (40 kph)

CONTACT

Invisible Structures, Inc.
1600 Jackson Street
Suite 310
Golden, CO 80401
Tel: 800-233-1510
www.invisible
structures.com
sales@invisible
structures.com

IMAGO

PLASTIC LAMINATE SHEETS WITH FABRIC AND PRINTED FILMS

Designed by Suzanne Tick and introduced by KnollTextiles in 2000, Imago is a family of products made through a patented process that encapsulates fabric in high-performance resin. The resulting hard surfaces combine the best qualities of fabric, resin, and glass, changing tone with the amount and direction of cast light, and thus affecting the perception of space beyond.

Introduced in 2003, ImagoPrints represent the next generation of translucent hard surface materials. Rather than incorporating actual fabrics, ImagoPrints use printed vellum-like layers to create visual depth and a "parallax effect," whereby the image appears to shift with the movement of the viewer. ImagoPrints patterns are created by the careful registration and printing of two customer-selected layer colors. Separated slightly from each other, the layers give the patterns a greater sense of depth and dimension.

Imago and ImagoPrints are half the weight of glass, scratch and fingerprint resistant, designed to withstand a variety of chemicals, maintained with common cleaning agents, and may be sawed, drilled, punched, riveted, bolted, hot-stamped, die-cut, thermoformed, and cold-bent. The material is available in six gauges, custom colors, custom surface textures, and a markerboard finish.

CONTENTS
Imago: PETG, fabric; ImagoPrints: Lexan, printed films

APPLICATIONS
Panels, screens, wallcoverings, markerboards, tabletops, window treatments, shelving, light diffuser lenses

TYPES / SIZES
4 × 8' (1.2 × 2.4 m) standard sheet size; 9 standard Imago patterns and 3 standard ImagoPrints available in 6 gauges from 1/16" (.2 cm) to 1/2" (1.3 cm) thick; custom patterns and a custom 4 × 10' (1.2 × 3 m) sheet size available

ENVIRONMENTAL
Recyclable

TESTS / EXAMINATIONS
Technical information available upon request

LIMITATIONS
Not recommended for exterior use

CONTACT
KnollTextiles
76 Ninth Avenue
New York, NY 10011
Tel: 718-230-8032
www.knolltextiles.com

INTELLIGENT PRODUCT

BIOMORPHIC SEATING UNIT

Jakob + MacFarlane, the Paris-based architects known for their Georges Restaurant at the top of the Centre Pompidou, have designed a form of seating called "It," which is inspired by organic structures. Made from hand-shaped and fire-lacquered resins with a high-gloss finish, It seating has a complex curvilinear form, which is perforated with nearly spherical voids for lightness and rigidity.

CONTENTS
Fiberglass, cold foamed
resins, car lacquer

APPLICATIONS
Seating

TYPES / SIZES
90.5 × 79 × 59"
(230 × 200 × 150 cm)

LIMITATIONS
Not for exterior use

CONTACT
Sawaya & Moroni
Via Andegari, 18
Milan, 20121
Italy
Tel: +39 02 8639218
www.sawayamoroni.com
info@sawayamoroni.com

RECYCLED POLYETHYLENE SHEET

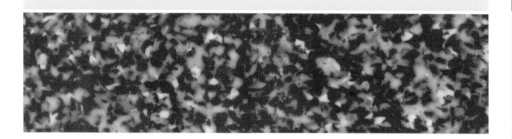

Jazz is comprised of off-cuts and used chopping boards from the food-preparation industry. Originally coded according to their use, Jazz sheets can be made from any combination and ratio of red, brown, blue, green, yellow, white, and black.

CONTENTS
100% recycled high molecular weight polyethylene

APPLICATIONS
Work surfaces, furniture, backsplashes, shower surrounds

TYPES / SIZES
79 × 39.5" (200 × 100 cm) panels, 1/2–1" (1.2–2.5 cm) thick

ENVIRONMENTAL
100% recycled content

CONTACT
Smile Plastics Ltd.
Mansion House, Ford
Shrewsbury, SY5 9LZ UK
Tel: +01743 850267
www.smile-plastics.co.uk
smileplas@aol.com

REPURPOSED MATERIAL

KRYSTAL WEAVE LAMINATES

TRANSLUCENT FABRIC ENCAPSULATED IN POLYMER RESIN SHEETS

Developed by Libby Kowalski, Krystal Weave Laminates capture and isolate fabrics from her Krystal Weave collection in transparent, shatterproof, fire-resistant sheets. The water-clear yarn-based fabrics are pressed between polymer sheets of various thicknesses. The panels may be cut and drilled with standard woodworking tools. Krystal Weave Laminates may be backlit, framed, or attached directly to a wall surface.

CONTENTS
Panel: 100% polymer resin; Fabric: 85% polymer, 10% nylon, 5% polyester

APPLICATIONS
Interior vertical surfaces, space dividers, windows, doors, cabinets, decorative wall treatments, signage

TYPES / SIZES
4 × 8' (1.2 × 2.4 m) and 4 × 10' (1.2 × 3 m) panels in thicknesses from 3/16" (.5 cm) to 1/2" (1.3 cm)

ENVIRONMENTAL
Some recycled resin material

LIMITATIONS
Limited exterior use

CONTACT
Kova Textiles, LLC
32 Union Square East
Suite 216
New York, NY 10003
Tel: 212-254-7591
www.kovatextiles.com
info@kovatextiles.com

CUSTOM-COLORED RECYCLED POLYMER PANELS

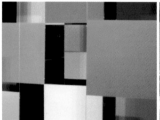

LightBlocks panels are a patented, durable, light-transmitting medium used for partitions, ceilings, furniture, doors, lighting fixtures, flooring, and sculpture. MB Wellington Studio utilizes a variety of clear polymer materials and applies a matte finish and fingerprint-block coating to them.

Color is completely custom at no extra cost, and there is no minimum order number or time delay. MB Wellington Studio will match Pantone colors, paint chips, etc. and can vary the amount of translucency within the material. Polymers are chosen based on recycled content, fire rating, LEED certification, or bulletproof requirements.

CONTENTS
Various polymers based on requirements

APPLICATIONS
Partitions, ceilings, furniture, doors, lighting fixtures, flooring, sculptures

TYPES / SIZES
4 × 8' (1.2 × 2.4 m) standard sheets; custom sizes available

ENVIRONMENTAL
Uses recycled plastics (MB Wellington Studio has recycled 50,000 lbs of scrap to date, 22,680 kg), will accept returned materials at the end of a project and recycle them

TESTS / EXAMINATIONS
Fire rated material on request

CONTACT
MB Wellington Studio, Inc.
141 Canal Street
Nashua, NH 03064
Tel: 603-889-1115
www.lightblocks.com
info@lightblocks.com

LIQUIDS GHOSTS

N° 102113-001

PLASTIC LAMINATE INCORPORATING MICROSCOPIC PHOTOGRAPHY

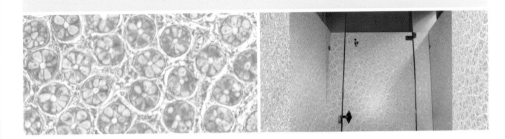

Alex Schweder created Liquids Ghosts in order to blur the distinction between buildings and the bodies that occupy them. His custom-designed plastic laminate, which consists of decorative surface papers impregnated with melamine resin and pressed over Kraft paper core sheets impregnated with phenolic resin, incorporates photographs of colon cells intended for restroom stall applications. The floral pattern of the colon's microscopic structure simultaneously provides reassurance through conventional architectural patterns and something unsettling.

CONTENTS
Paper, melamine, and phenolic resins

APPLICATIONS
Furniture, casework, decorative surfacing on restroom stalls, columns, wainscoting, valances, cornices, interior doors, divider systems

TYPES / SIZES
Sheet widths: 36" (91.5 cm), 48" (122 cm)
Sheet Lengths: 96–120" (244–305 cm), 144" (366 cm)

TESTS / EXAMINATIONS
NEMA

CONTACT
Wilsonart International
2400 Wilson Place
PO Box 6110
Temple, TX 76503
Tel: 206-624-8603
www.stinehourpress.com

LIQUID-INFUSED TABLES, SURFACES, AND FLOOR TILES

With the aim of developing interactive environments, Gianfranco Barban and Gregg Brodarick of B.lab have created a series of tabletop surfaces and floor tiles, which are made of layers of plastic sheets encapsulating nontoxic liquids. These liquids move and bubble in various ways based on touch, depicting constantly changing patterns.

The bichromatic floor tiles generate colorful forms in continuous evolution, so walking on the tiles leaves a trail of footprints. These tiles are comprised of two shock-resistant layers of PVC, and the upper layer is treated with a nonslip surface. Welded together, the layers create a rigid tile.

CONTENTS
Living Surfaces: acrylic top with MDF wood base and aluminum or wood edge; Living Floor: 100% PVC floor tiles containing non-toxic colored liquids

APPLICATIONS
Horizontal surfaces and floor tiles

TYPES / SIZES
Table top dimensions: 24 × 31.5 × 39.5" (60 × 80 × 100 cm), round or square; tile dimensions 2 × 2 × .3" (5 × 5 × .7 cm), 4 × 4 × .3" (10 × 10 × .7 cm)

TESTS / EXAMINATIONS
Chair test EN425

LIMITATIONS
Not for exterior use

CONTACT
B.lab Italia
Via Marmolada 20
Gallarate, 21013
Italy
Tel: +39 0331 774445
www.blabitalia.com
living@blabitalia.com

TRANSFORMATIONAL PRODUCT

RECOMBINANT PRODUCT

LUMICAST

HAND-CAST RESIN PANELS WITH ENCAPSULATED 3D OBJECTS

Lumicast incorporates embedded materials such as textiles, fibers, and organic substances within hand-cast polyester resin panels. Various inks and geometric patterns may also be added in combinations of opaque, tinted, and translucent layers. Unlike manufactured products, the finished result is a site-specific, handmade piece of artwork.

CONTENTS
Polyester resin, encapsulated material

APPLICATIONS
Wall panels, space dividers, artwork

TYPES / SIZES
55 × 117 × 3/4" (140 × 297 × 1.9 cm) maximum dimensions; variety of finishes and tints available

LIMITATIONS
Not recommended for horizontal, exterior, or wet applications

CONTACT
Skyline Design, Inc.
1240 North Homan Avenue
Chicago, IL 60651
Tel: 888-278-4660
www.skydesign.com
sales@skydesign.com

TRANSLUCENT RESIN WITH ENCAPSULATED MATERIALS

Lumicor's patented technology creates a new class of material by combining the beauty of natural botanicals, fine textiles, decorative papers, glass, metal, and stone within a choice of high performance resins. Lumicor provides exceptional depth and clarity and outstanding UV properties. It is a lightweight, high-strength material that is easy to fabricate and install and may be recycled.

CONTENTS
100% high performance resins plus interlayer

APPLICATIONS
Furniture, lighting, partitions, sink bowls, vanity tops, table tops, shower enclosures, signage, displays, cabinet doors, column wraps, door inserts, ceiling panels, interior windows, acoustical panels

TYPES / SIZES
4 × 8' (1.2 × 2.4 m) and 5 × 10' (1.5 × 3 m) sheets, with thicknesses from 1/16" (.2 cm) to 1" (2.5 cm)

ENVIRONMENTAL
Recyclable

TESTS / EXAMINATIONS
ASTM E84 Class B rating, suitable for interior use

CONTACT
Lumicor
1400 Monster Road Southwest
Renton, WA 98055
Tel: 425-255-4000
www.lumicor.com
sales@lumicor.com

RECOMBINANT PRODUCT

LUMISTY

LIGHT-FILTERING POLYESTER FILM

Lumisty first drew widespread attention when it was used on the windows of Pleats Please, Issey Miyake's clothing boutique in SoHo.

Upon first encountering the product, people are often struck by what seems like an optical illusion. Walking past a window with Lumisty applied, a perfectly clear, transparent glass surface becomes partially fogged. Two or three steps later, the same window is completely fogged. As the viewer's angle shifts, so does the transparency or translucency of the film.

CONTENTS
99% polyester film, 1% acrylic pressure-sensitive adhesive

APPLICATIONS
Glazing film for store fronts, showrooms, room dividers

TYPES / SIZES
4.1 × 49.2' (1.25 × 15 m) roll

ENVIRONMENTAL
Blocks 98% of UV, enhances durability of substrate

LIMITATIONS
Not for exterior application

CONTACT
Madico Inc. / GlassFilm Enterprises Inc.
45 Industrial Parkway
Woburn, MA 01888
Tel: 978-263-9333
www.lumistyfilm.com

OCEAN SERIES

FIBERGLASS SCULPTURE FOR PUBLIC SEATING

Tom Yglesias's Ocean Series polyester and fiberglass sculptures are designed for public seating in exterior and interior environments. The sculptures are designed to be monumental centerpieces for open spaces such as plazas or landscapes. Ocean Series sculptures are also available in cast bronze.

CONTENTS
85% polyester resin, 15% fiberglass (cast bronze also available)

APPLICATIONS
Public seating

TYPES / SIZES
20–24' (6.1–7.3 m) long, 3' (.9 m) wide, 3' (.9 m) high

CONTACT
Crest Company
434 Estado Way
Novado, CA 94945
Tel: 415-892-0055
www.creststudio.com
oceanseries@aol.com

REPURPOSED MATERIAL

ORIGINS

RECYCLED POLYETHYLENE PANELS

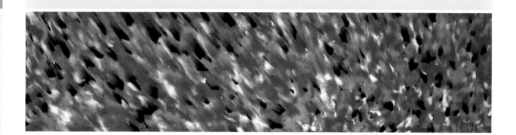

Origins one hundred percent postconsumer recycled polyethylene panels provide an alternative to virgin polyethylene versions. Origins panels possess virtually identical properties compared with virgin panels, and they are available in numerous colors and patterns, including custom patterns.

Origins material is primarily comprised of translucent one-gallon milk jugs, which are collected locally and processed by grinding, washing, and forming the plastic into pellets. These pellets are transformed into plastic resin, which may be further processed or directly pressed into panels.

CONTENTS
100% postconsumer recycled polyethylene

APPLICATIONS
Restroom partitions, store fixtures, furniture, specialty products

TYPES / SIZES
2 × 4' (.6 × 1.2 m), 4 × 8' (1.2 × 2.4 m); 5 × 10' (1.5 × 3 m) panels, 1/8–2" (.3–5 cm) thick

ENVIRONMENTAL
100% recycled material, recyclable

LIMITATIONS
Structural or exterior uses should be carefully engineered

CONTACT
Yemm & Hart Ltd.
1417 Madison 308
Marquand, MO 63655
Tel: 573-783-5434
www.yemmhart.com
yemmhart@earthlink.net

TRANSLUCENT HONEYCOMB PANELS WITH LAMINATED FIBERGLASS OR CAST RESIN FACINGS

Panelite panels were developed by architects Emmanuelle Bourlier and Christian Mitman to resolve an architectural design challenge. The panels use a sandwich construction typically exploited in the aerospace industry for its high strength-to-weight ratio and excellent resistance to deflection. The structural honeycomb core provides strength and consistent rigidity at a very low density: when bonded to similarly lightweight facings, every honeycomb cell wall acts like the web of an I-beam, forming an extremely strong, stiff, yet lightweight, composite panel. With translucent facings the honeycomb panel becomes a versatile building material: a lightweight, rigid panel offering a range of aesthetic, textural, and light effects.

Due to their cast facings, Cast Polymer Series panels offer a superior bond strength-making them suitable for light load-bearing applications such as countertops, tables, workstations, and display pedestals. They also offer a unique range of custom and refined detailing options, including nearly unlimited colors, self-sealed edges, integral mitered corners, pre-applied interlocking hardware for installation-ready self-supporting walls, and curved radii ranging from six inches to ninety-six feet.

Panelite panels may be used to provide varying degrees of visual privacy and to transmit, pixelate, color, or diffuse light, allowing designers to conceive the use of light, texture, and spatial definition in innovative ways. The panels can be cut, drilled, and machined using standard wood-working methods and tools. Panelite Laminated Series and Cast Resin panels are U.S. patent protected.

CONTENTS

Core: aluminum hexagonal, aluminum overexpanded, or tubular polycarbonate honeycomb. Facings: fiberglass or cast polyester resin

APPLICATIONS

Flat or curved interior vertical surfaces, including partition walls and sliding, pivoting or hinged doors; exhibit, display, and signage; ceilings

TYPES / SIZES

4 × 8' (1.2 × 2.4 m) or 4 × 10' (1.2 × 3 m) sheets; Laminated series: clear or blue fiberglass; Cast Resin series: seven standard colors plus custom colors

ENVIRONMENTAL

Recyclable components, support natural daylighting, efficient use of materials

TESTS / EXAMINATIONS

Flammability rating ASTM E84 Class C

LIMITATIONS

Not for exterior use

CONTACT

Panelite
3341 La Cienega Place
Los Angeles, CA 90016
Tel: 310-202-1115
www.panelite.us
info@panelite.us

EXPANDED POLYPROPYLENE ACOUSTICAL PANELS

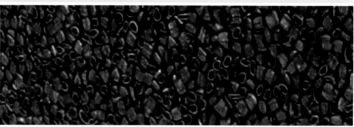

Pepp acoustical panels are made with ARPRO, which is expanded polypropylene bead foam. Pepp panels are lightweight, structurally rigid, and are resistant to fire, water, and bacteria. Pepp panels make an ideal acoustic treatment and tackable surface for conference rooms, environmentally sensitive areas, performance spaces, classrooms, swimming pools, skating rinks, etc.

Pepp is resistant to oils, grease, and most chemicals and is washable with a power washer. Pepp is available in charcoal or white and may also be painted. Pepp one-inch panels provide an NRC rating of 0.55, and two-inch-thick panels provide an NRC rating of 0.70.

CONTENTS
100% polypropylene

APPLICATIONS
Acoustic treatment for interior vertical surfaces and ceilings, tack board

TYPES / SIZES
2 × 4' (.6 × 1.2 m) panels, 1" (2.5 cm) or 2" (5 cm) thick

ENVIRONMENTAL
Mold and bacteria resistant

TESTS / EXAMINATIONS
ASTM E84 "Class A" fire retardant

LIMITATIONS
Not for exterior use; not to be used as flooring or horizontal surfacing

CONTACT
Robin Reigi Inc.
48 West 21st Street
New York, NY 10010
Tel: 212-924-5558
www.robin-reigi.com
info@robin-reigi.com

HPL TOOL-FREE TABLE

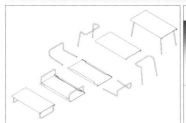

Matthias Demacker's design for the Plug.table represents the ultimate reduction of an object to its essence. The table is made of three parts, a high-pressure laminate tabletop and two stainless steel legframes, and it may be assembled and modified without any tools. Plug.table may be configured to be either counter or coffee table height based on the insertion orientation of the legframes.

Plug.table utilizes the postforming process of compact-forming HPL, and the table surface may be produced in a variety of colors. The table is suitable for interior or exterior use, and multiple tables may be connected by interlocking the legframes.

CONTENTS
Tabletop: compact-forming high-pressure laminate, legs: stainless steel

APPLICATIONS
Furniture

TYPES / SIZES
31.5 × 47" (80 × 120 cm),
31.5 × 63" (80 × 160 cm),
31.5 × 75" (80 × 190 cm),
31.5 × 88.5" (80 × 225 cm)

ENVIRONMENTAL
Minimal use of materials

CONTACT
Habit
Ulrich Loholz GmbH,
Im Heider Feld 2
Kuerten-Engeldorf, 51515
Germany
Tel: +49 (0) 2207 81134
www.habit.de

ULTRAPERFORMING PRODUCT

SCINTILLA

LIGHT-REACTIVE POLYMER

Made of a light conducting matrix embedded within a substrate, SensiTiles transport light from one surface point to another by a process called "total internal reflection," the same principle that makes fiber optics possible. SensiTiles either respond to shadows or an active and moving light source. In the former case, SensiTiles cause any shadows that fall on their surfaces to shift. In the latter, they redirect and scatter any oncoming light. In an environment with ambient light, shadow-producing movements around a SensiTile will produce a rippling effect. In darker environments, beams of light are redirected to emerge from another part of the surface.

SensiTiles also absorb and "bleed" colors. If colored light falls on a SensiTile, echoes of that color are dispersed throughout its surface. If multiple colors are present, they become blended, rearranged, and scrambled. Because SensiTile's properties are inherent, no power is required; the light effects are created passively from external light sources, and they last as long as the material does. SensiTile is available in different substrates that each lend distinctive properties to the material. Scintilla incorporates a translucent acrylic polymer, giving the tiles a very high density of light-reactive points. Scintilla is available in a variety of standard and custom colors. (See also SensiTile Terrazzo, which is embedded in concrete.)

CONTENTS
100% PMMA (polymethyl methacrylate)

APPLICATIONS
Decorative surfacing material for vertical and horizontal applications

TYPES / SIZES
4 × 4" (10 × 10 cm), 4 × 8" (10 × 20 cm), 8 × 8" (20 × 20 cm) tiles in 1/2" (1.3 cm) thickness; 6 × 6" (15 × 15 cm), 6 × 12" (15 × 30.5 cm), 12 × 12" (30.5 × 30.5 cm) tiles in 1-1/2" (4 cm) thickness; corner tiles also available; custom colors available

ENVIRONMENTAL
No power required for responsive effect

CONTACT
SensiTile Systems
1604 Clay Avenue, 3rd Floor
Detroit, MI 48211
Tel: 313-872-6314
www.sensitile.com
info@sensitile.com

SMARTWRAP

CUSTOMIZABLE PRINT FACADE OR INTERIOR WALL MATERIAL

SmartWrap was featured at the inaugural SOLOS exhibit at the Cooper Hewitt National Design Museum. KieranTimberlake designed SmartWrap to be the building envelope of the future: a composite that integrates the segregated functions of a conventional wall and combines them into one single product. Inspired by material science and the printing industry, SmartWrap utilizes innovative products printed onto fabric and plastic film in a roll-to-roll or deposition process. The idea is realized through the transfer of technologies from other industries to provide the following criteria: shelter, climate control, lighting, information display, and power.

CONTENTS

PET, OLED, OTFB, OPV, OTFC, PCM, other customizable organic and sustainable products

APPLICATIONS

Exterior or interior walls for information, light-emission, power

ENVIRONMENTAL

Recyclable, organic, efficient use of material

CONTACT

KieranTimberlake Associates LLP 420 North 20th Street Philadelphia, PA 19310 Tel: 215-922-6600 x100 www.kierantimberlake.com

MULTIDIMENSIONAL PRODUCT

SOUNDWAVE

POLYESTER ACOUSTIC PANELS

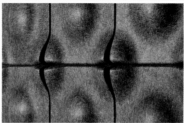

Soundwave was designed by Teppo Asikainen to help control the sound levels in busy interiors. Made from recyclable molded polyester-fiber, which is the same material used in the auto industry to reduce noise levels in car interiors, the undulating wave form and the feltlike material of the panel helps reduce noise levels by absorbing the mid to high frequency range.

Swell and Scrunch panels are to be used as lightweight sound absorbers in the upper frequency range (500 Hz and above). The Diffuser panel provides not sound absorption but sound diffusion: in the proper position, it will improve speech intelligibility and even improve privacy in open spaces. The Luna panel is a Class A broadband absorber with extended efficiency in the low frequency range (150-500 Hz) and is therefore very efficient in reducing background noise.

CONTENTS
Polyester fiber, felt, PET

APPLICATIONS
Acoustic treatment for interior vertical surfaces and ceilings

TYPES / SIZES
Swell, Swell Diffuser, Scrunch, Luna; 22.8 × 22.8 × 3.1" (58 × 58 × 7.9 cm)

ENVIRONMENTAL
Recyclable, low embodied energy

TESTS / EXAMINATIONS
Sound absorption Class A: EN ISO 11654

LIMITATIONS
Not for exterior use

CONTACT
Offecct AB
Skovdevagen, Box 100
Tibro, SE-543 21 Sweden
Tel: +46 (0)504 415 00
www.offecct.se

PRESSURE-INFLATED ETFE FOIL SYSTEMS

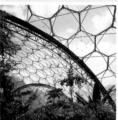

Foiltec's Texlon foil system offers designers new opportunities in the development of climatic and transparent envelopes. The system can be engineered to virtually any size or shape and can incorporate variable solar and thermal controls, enabling the envelope to be tuned to the ideal climatic or programmatic solution in real time as the sun moves across the sky. Made of a fluoroplastic film, the Texlon system is self-cleaning and will not deteriorate with UV exposure. It is also engineered to withstand specific and local snow and wind loads.

The Texlon foil elements are stabilized by a slight overpressure between the individual layers of foil. The air-filled elements prevent the foil from becoming slack and provide the system with its excellent thermal properties. However, the air is not part of the structural system, as in the case of air-inflated buildings, where a breakdown in the air supply would cause the entire structure to collapse. With the Texlon system, a breakdown in the air supply would only affect the thermal properties, and the building would remain intact.

CONTENTS
ETFE foil, aluminum
perimeter frames

APPLICATIONS
Roof systems, wall systems,
skylights

ENVIRONMENTAL
Low embodied energy,
high strength-to-weight
ratio, intelligent day-
lighting, system
recyclability, longevity

CONTACT
Foiltec NA
13 Green Mountain Drive
Cohoes, NY 12047
Tel: 518-783-0575
www.foiltec.com
info@foiltecna.com

CURVILINEAR SUSPENDED CEILING SYSTEM

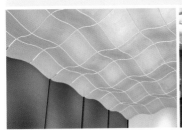  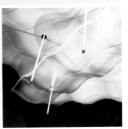

The Topo 3D System transforms flat ceiling planes into uniquely expressive undulating landscapes full of form, dimension, and color.

The system consists of preformed translucent and opaque Lexan infill panels installed into a curved suspension system. The infill panels are designed in four-panel modules to create the appearance of gently rolling curves.

The visual impact of the system can be enhanced through independently supported lighting, which may be used to highlight the panel's soft, translucent colors. Lighting and utilities are easily integrated into the system through optional utility circles (four-inch diameter), which are positioned either at the high or low points of the suspension system intersections or centered on individual panels.

The Lexan panels are installed into the precurved Donn Brand Topo Suspension System, a narrow-profile (9/16-inch wide) extruded aluminum suspension system, which is offered in coordinated colors to complement the panel finishes.

CONTENTS
Lexan panels

APPLICATIONS
Ceilings

TYPES / SIZES
2 × 2' (.6 ×.6 m) panels, TOPO System 12: 12" (30.5 cm) depth, TOPO System 8: 8" (20 cm) depth; 5 standard colors: clear translucent, blue translucent, glass green translucent, white translucent and white opaque; custom colors available

TESTS / EXAMINATIONS
ASTM E84 Class A rated

CONTACT
USG Interiors, Inc.
125 South Franklin Street
Chicago, IL 60606
Tel: 800-874-4968
www.usg.com
usg4you@usg.com

LUMINOUS ACRYLIC CEILING PANELS

Translucents acrylic infill panels add visual interest and luminosity to ceiling design. The panels accommodate both curved and flat ceiling systems and can be integrated with lighting to create a variety of visual effects from soft, diffused looks to bolder, more dramatic treatments.

For curved ceiling applications, the panels can be installed as part of USG's Curvatura 3D ceiling system. This system consists of precurved grid components that snap together quickly and easily. For flat ceilings, the panels are ideal for use in the company's Gridware suspension system or Donn brand DX and DXT suspension systems.

CONTENTS
Acrylic panels, steel frame

APPLICATIONS
Ceilings

TYPES / SIZES
2 × 2' (.6 × .6 m) panels,
custom sizes up to 4 × 12'
(1.2 × 3.7 m); Lexan clear
matte, Lexan glass green
matte, or FRP natural finish

TESTS / EXAMINATIONS
ASTM E84 Class A rated

LIMITATIONS
For interior use only

CONTACT
USG Interiors, Inc.
125 South Franklin Street
Chicago, IL 60606
Tel: 800-874-4968
www.usg.com
usg4you@usg.com

MULTIDIMENSIONAL PRODUCT

UNDERCOVER TABLE

POLYCARBONATE TABLE THAT TRANSFORMS INTO AN EMERGENCY SHELTER

Thom Faulders and Anna Rainer designed the Undercover Table to provide protection and supplies to building occupants during an earthquake. Adaptable to other natural and man-made disasters, the table rests compact and compressed during everyday usage, yet is designed to "spring into action" when necessary. Providing a safe haven amidst unpredictable chaos, the tanks within the Undercover Table are designed to efficiently deliver their comfort and emergency supplies as one dives underneath.

The Undercover Table represents the discovery of a use for what is generally considered "nonproductive" space; the table relies on the zone below its surface for its functional and aesthetic significance. The oblong shape of the storage tanks is derived from the residual space between a sitter's knees and the underside of the table top. Clearly visible from above through the translucent polycarbonate surface, the brightly colored tanks are wrapped in protective bands and provide a blurred and vibrant pattern, which is highly visible during a disaster.

The perforated protective bands disengage from the tanks to be reconnected and stuffed with foraged soft items to form cushions for reclining and sleeping. Designed with maximum flexibility in mind, these bands may also be used as clothing wraps, slings, or handbags. In addition, the tabletop may be disengaged from the frame to become a stretcher with handholds.

CONTENTS
Polycarbonate, steel, vinyl, nylon, emergency supplies

APPLICATIONS
Residential use

TYPES / SIZES
30 × 72 × 39"
(76 × 183 × 99 cm)

ENVIRONMENTAL
Designed for use during an emergency

LIMITATIONS
Prototype

CONTACT
Beige Design
1025 Carleton Street #14
Berkeley, CA 94710
Tel: 510-666-0892
www.beigedesign.com

INTERLAYERS FUSED WITH ECORESIN

3form's Varia is a panel system comprised of decorative interlayers encapsulated within one hundred percent ecoresin. As its name implies, the design choices for Varia resin panels are varied and diverse: 3form allows custom selection of the color, pattern, texture, interlayer, and finish for the material. Ecoresin is the primary binding agent, developed exclusively by 3form with partner Bayer and Eastman Corporation to be an environmentally positive composite commonly identified as co-polyester.

CONTENTS

Ecoresin, interlayers (fabrics, papers, organics, etc.)

APPLICATIONS

Wall paneling, balustrades, work surfaces, decorative treatments, furniture, exterior surfaces, light diffusers, ceiling panels, signage, acoustical panels

TYPES / SIZES

4 × 8' (1.2 × 2.4 m) and 4 × 10' (1.2 × 3 m) panels, 1/16" (.2 cm) to 1" (2.5 cm) thick

ENVIRONMENTAL

Contains 40% recycled material, recyclable

TESTS / EXAMINATIONS

ASTM E84 Class B rating

CONTACT

3form
2300 South 2300 West
Suite B
Salt Lake City, UT 84119
Tel: 801-649-2500
www.3-form.com

WATERCONE

POLYCARBONATE SOLAR WATER PURIFIER

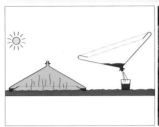  

Roughly twenty percent of the world's population faces a daily challenge in finding an adequate supply of drinking water. In most developing countries, women and children spend a major part of the day procuring drinking water for the family.

Designed by Stephan Augustin, the Watercone is intended to provide potable water to populations who desperately need it. The Watercone is a conical, self-supporting and stackable unit made from transparent, thermo-formable polycarbonate (the same material used for water dispensers), outfitted with a screw cap spout at the tip, as well as an inward circular collecting trough at the base. Technically speaking, the Watercone is a solar still.

Based on an average evaporation level of 8.8 liters per square meter, the Watercone yields between 1.0 to 1.5 liters of condensed water per day, and can be referred to as a one-step water condensation process with a forty percent effectiveness rating.

When salty or brackish water is inserted in the Watercone, it evaporates by way of solar irradiation, and the condensation appears in the form of droplets on the inner wall of the cone. These droplets trickle down the inner wall into a circular trough at the inner base of the cone. By unscrewing the cap at the tip of the cone and turning the cone upside down, one can empty the potable water gathered in the trough directly into a drinking device.

Augustin's Watercone provides a simple and inexpensive solution to an age-old problem: turning salt water into potable water.

CONTENTS
100% polycarbonate

APPLICATIONS
Coastal arid areas with mainly sea water or brackish well water

TYPES / SIZES
Diameter 31.5" (80 cm), height 12" (30 cm), weight about 4.4 lbs (2 kg)

ENVIRONMENTAL
Makes potable water available to needy populations, nontoxic, and fully recyclable material

TESTS / EXAMINATIONS
German TUV tested in India based on WHO Water standards

CONTACT
Augustin Produktentwicklung
Tengstasse 45
D-80796 Munich
Germany
Tel: +49-(0)89-2730690
www.watercone.com

ILLUMINATING POLYCARBONATE TABLES

Conceived by Sebastian Bergne as a family of lamps for Luceplan, Zia, Zio, and Nipotino are discreet pieces of furniture that also function as light fixtures. Unencumbered by excess, the lamps' shapes are clean, light, and minimal due to the absence of a cable, which is passed through the leg of the table. A fluorescent lamp is placed beneath the white polycarbonate surface and casts a soft and diffused light.

Zia is a round table, capable of supporting the weight of relatively heavy objects such as books, a plant, or a serving tray. A sophisticated system allows for it to be switched on using a touch-sensitive switch placed on its surface. Zia can also be used as a bedside table.

Zio was conceived as a desk lamp, and it is smaller and rectangular in shape. Its slightly inclined surface allows for the tidy gathering of papers, which often litter desks.

The smallest of the three, Nipotino, is a simple rectangular desk lamp, which can be used next to computer keyboards.

CONTENTS
100% UV-resistant
polycarbonate

APPLICATIONS
Furniture, lighting

TYPES / SIZES
Zia: diameter 19.5 × 12"
(50 × 30 cm); Zio: 14 ×
10.5 × 12" (35 × 27 × 30 cm);
Nipotino: 14.5 × 4.5 × 4"
(37 × 12 × 10 cm)

ENVIRONMENTAL
Recycled material

CONTACT
Luceplan Spa
Via E.T. Moneta 46
Milan, 20161
Italy
Tel: +39 2 662421
www.luceplan.com

FAUX LEATHER

RUBBER FLOOR AND WALL TILES

These rubber tiles are a frugal alternative to real leather, and are far more abrasion-resistant than leather. Rubber sheets are butt-jointed together and adhered to a substrate with a dual component epoxy or polyurethane adhesive. The sheets must be trimmed around the perimeter for a clean edge. Regular maintenance with soap and water as well as waxing is recommended.

CONTENTS
100% rubber

APPLICATIONS
Floor tiles, wall tiles, benches, tabletops, substitute for leather in any application it is used

TYPES / SIZES
Nominal size of the panel is 39 × 39 × 1/8" (99 × 99 × .3 cm) thick; this panel must be trimmed to a maximum of 36 × 36" (91.5 × 91.5 cm)

ENVIRONMENTAL
Longer lasting than leather, no animal by-products

LIMITATIONS
These panels must be trimmed before installation; not fire rated; not for exterior use

CONTACT
Robin Reigi Inc.
48 West 21st Street
New York, NY 10010
Tel: 212-924-5558
www.robin-reigi.com
info@robin-reigi.com

MORPHING TRANSPARENT SURFACE

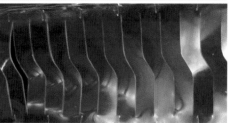

Developed by Soo-in Yang and David Benjamin, Kinetic Glass is a responsive surface that reacts to environmental conditions and changes shape via curling or opening and closing gills. The surface is thin, lightweight, and transparent with no motors or mechanical parts.

The system may be used with a variety of switches or sensors and controlled via microprocessors and complex algorithms, allowing one to perform a variety of applications. In one case, the system can detect unhealthy levels of carbon dioxide in interior spaces. Kinetic Glass "breathes" when high levels are encountered, enhancing air movement and signaling the problem to building occupants.

CONTENTS
Cured urethane rubber, shape memory alloy

APPLICATIONS
"Breathing" window, bending wall, adaptive curtain

TYPES / SIZES
24 × 12" (61 × 30.5 cm) panel, with 8 wires and 16 slits; custom dimensions and shapes possible

ENVIRONMENTAL
Automated environmental control

LIMITATIONS
Not yet tested for exterior use

CONTACT
The Living
277 West 11 Street, #1A
New York, NY 10014
www.thelivingnewyork.com

TRANSFORMATIONAL MATERIAL

WELLIES

RECYCLED CHILDREN'S BOOTS

Children grow out of their Wellington boots quickly, and thousands of pairs end up unsold in charity shops and eventually disappear into landfill sites with other garbage. Smile Plastics has managed to divert these boots from the waste stream; by a process of heat and up to one thousand tons of pressure, the boots are pressed into four-millimeter-thick sheets. Soft, rubbery, and tactile, the sheets are ideal for table coverings, bar and barstool tops, or even as waterproof mats for bathrooms and kitchens.

CONTENTS
100% recycled rubber

APPLICATIONS
Wall coverings, tapestries, floor mats

TYPES / SIZES
47 × 31.5" (120 x 80 cm) panels
.2" (.4 cm) thick

ENVIRONMENTAL
100% recycled content

CONTACT
Smile Plastics Ltd.
Mansion House, Ford
Shrewsbury, SY5 9LZ UK
Tel: +01743 850267
www.smile-plastics.co.uk
smileplas@aol.com

06: **GLASS**

BUBBLE GLASS

SHEET GLASS CONTAINING GRIDS AND PATTERNS OF BUBBLES

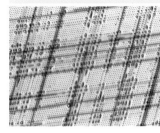  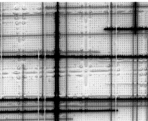

Developed by Penny Herscovitch and Dan Gottlieb, Bubble Glass contains perfect grids of tiny bubbles and a variety of bubble patterns. Bubble Glass originated during PadLAb's 2004 architectural glass commission for a residence on the coast of Brazil. While attempting to create a colorful mesh pattern in glass, the team discovered the Bubble Glass technique, which involves fusing multiple layers of glass in a kiln.

Fascinated by the magic of designing with air trapped inside glass, PadLab looked to traditional styles of Swedish glass blowing for further inspiration. Based on this research, they developed a process of controlling bubbles to form images and even text within flat glass. Although the manufacturer controls the patterns of trapped air, each piece of Bubble Glass is unique.

CONTENTS
100% glass (with controlled air bubbles)

APPLICATIONS
Lighting, interior room dividers, privacy window and door panels, tabletops, functional objects and fine art; can be slumped

TYPES / SIZES
1/4" (.6 cm)-thick panels up to 6 ft² (.56 m²); standard sheets are clear with a grid of tiny bubbles; custom colors, bubble patterns, and imagery available

ENVIRONMENTAL
No glues, laminates, lead, or toxic materials

LIMITATIONS
Must be tempered for use in applications that require safety glass

CONTACT
PadLAb
612 Moulton Ave #1
Los Angeles, CA 90031
Tel: 323-441-9189
www.padlab.com
pad@padlab.com

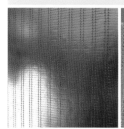

DECO WIRED GLASS

Glass

METAL WIRE–REINFORCED SAFETY GLASS

RECOMBINANT MATERIAL

Designed by Simone de Waart, Deco Wired Glass is safety glass reinforced with stainless steel wires knitted into decorative configurations. Because the wires are integrated with figured glass featuring a low-relief surface pattern, the three dimensional qualities of the material are intensified. The wire reinforcement is polished to keep it as inconspicuous as possible.

CONTENTS
Glass, stainless steel

APPLICATIONS
Partition walls, facade panels, double glazing, shower cubicles, back splashes, tabletops, doors, cupboard fronts

TYPES / SIZES
Plain 18 × 94.5" (45 × 240 cm); riffle 39 × 94.5" (100 × 240 cm); triply 39 × 94.5" (100 × 240 cm); minimum thickness .3" (.8 cm)

LIMITATIONS
Glass panels should be protected from moisture

CONTACT
Loods 5 Ontwerpers in cooperation with van Tetterode Glas Voorthuizen
Gen. Bothastraat 5k
Eindhoven, 5642 NJ
The Netherlands
www.loods5ont
werpers.com
loods5@chello.nl

GLASS SANDPAPER

CAST GLASS STAIR TREADS WITH SLIP-RESISTANT FINISH

Nathan Allan has developed a unique surface safety finish called Glass Sandpaper which provides an exceptional grip for shoe treads. Unlike other finishes that wear out quickly, Glass Sandpaper is durable and long lasting, and therefore ideal for cast glass stair treads and landings.

Treads can be produced in clear, crystal clear, textured, colored, or privacy-coated versions. There are forty-five current textures to choose from, as well as unlimited colors. Cast Glass Treads are easy to clean with hot water, ammonia, or special glass solutions.

CONTENTS
95% glass, 5% polyester resin

APPLICATIONS
Stair treads, landings, bridges, patio decks

TYPES / SIZES
1" (2.5 cm) thick consisting of two 1/2" (1.3 cm)-thick layers; can be produced in 2 or 3 layers, up to 2" (5.1 cm) thick

TESTS / EXAMINATIONS
ASTM D 2047-99 Coefficient of Friction Rating

CONTACT
Nathan Allan Glass Studios Inc.
110-12011 Riverside Way
Richmond, BC V6W 1K6
Canada
Tel: 604-277-8533 x225
www.nathanallan.com

TRANSPARENT PROJECTION SURFACE

Originally developed at the Institute for Light and Building Technology, HoloPro is a transparent rear projection surface that is almost completely unaffected by surrounding ambient light, and may even be used in daylit environments.

HoloPro consists of Holographic Optical Elements (HOE), which are exposed on a high resolution film through the use of a laser. The angle-based selectivity of the HOEs ensures that only the light emitted by a projector is directed toward the observer. Consequently, the ambient light coming from other directions passes directly through the screen and does not interfere with the projected images. The exposed and developed film is embedded between two pieces of transparent material for protection, and the assembly is UV stable for exterior use.

CONTENTS
Glass, polycarbonate, HOE

APPLICATIONS
Visual displays, signage, digital art

TYPES / SIZES
50" (127 cm) standard screen size

CONTACT
G+B Pronova GmbH
Lustheide 85
Bergisch Gladbach, 51427
Germany
Tel: +49 (0) 2204-204-301
www.holopro.com

INTELLIGENT MATERIAL

ICESTONE

DURABLE SURFACE MATERIAL MADE FROM RECYCLED GLASS AND CEMENT

 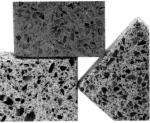 

IceStone's durable surfaces are terrazzolike composites made from up to seventy-five percent recycled glass and cement. By directing hundreds of tons of glass away from the waste stream, IceStone provides a sustainable alternative to nonrenewable and petrochemically derived materials.

IceStone is manufactured in a daylit factory in the Brooklyn Navy Yard by a company that values socially responsible business practices. Extremely resilient and available in a wide array of colors, IceStone durable surfaces may be used for a range of applications, such as countertops and floor and wall coverings.

IceStone durable surfaces are installed and maintained just like granite, and they may be easily cut, shaped, inlaid and mounted vertically or horizontally. Polishing brings out the luminescence of the glass, and honing or sandblasting adds texture and may further increase variations in shades and colors.

CONTENTS

Up to 75% recycled glass, white Portland cement

APPLICATIONS

Kitchen countertops, bathroom vanities, flooring, wall cladding, fireplace surrounds, conference tables, outdoor/indoor furniture, such as bistro tabletops

TYPES / SIZES

52.5 × 96" (133 × 244 cm) slabs of 1" (2.5 cm) thickness; 26 colors

ENVIRONMENTAL

All the glass used is recycled; the product is made in a daylit factory using a low-emissions manufacturing process

TESTS / EXAMINATIONS

ASTM C-97, C-109, C-293, C-642, C-666, C-1028, C-1260

CONTACT

IceStone LLC
63 Flushing Avenue
Unit 283
Brooklyn, NY 11205
Tel: 718-624-4900
www.icestone.biz
info@icestone.biz

CAPILLARY DAYLIGHTING GLASS

Kapilux is an insulating glass with an integrated capillary slab consisting of a large number of honeycomb-structured thin-walled transparent or white capillaries. This capillary slab can be integrated into different kinds of insulating glass, and it diffuses light effectively. Energy transmission, light transmission, and light diffusion can be adapted to the facade orientation and the room behind the facade.

CONTENTS
Glass, thermal control coatings

APPLICATIONS
Daylight control

ENVIRONMENTAL
Increases energy efficiency, reduces glare

LIMITATIONS
Limited visibility

CONTACT
Okalux GmbH
Am Jospershecklein 1
Marktheidenfeld, 97828
Germany
Tel: +49 9391 9000
www.okalux.de
info@okalux.de

LIVING GLASS

TABLES AND OBJECTS WITH FRACTURED GLASS SURFACES

  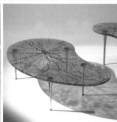 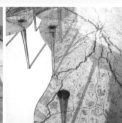

Gianfranco Barban and Gregg Brodarick of B.lab have created a series of tabletops, panels, and floor tiles they call Living Glass. To create the product, they seal a sheet of tempered glass between layers of plastic, and shatter the glass to render an explosion of sparkling fragments. These panels are produced in a variety of sizes, thicknesses, and colors.

CONTENTS
Glass and colored resins

APPLICATIONS
Coffee tables, floor tiles, horizontal and vertical surfaces

TYPES / SIZES
Tables: 23.5 × 31.5 × 39.5" (60 × 80 × 100 cm), 31.5 × 31.5 × 39.5" (80 × 80 × 100 cm), 23.5 × 47 × 39.5" (60 × 120 × 100 cm)
Horizontal surfaces: maximum sheet size 39.5 × 94.5" (100 × 240 cm)
Floor and wall tiles: 16 × 16" (40 × 40 cm); 16 × 31.5" (40 × 80 cm)
Not for exterior use

CONTACT
B.lab Italia
Via Marmolada 20
Gallarate, 21013 Italy
Tel: +39 0331 774445
www.blabitalia.com
living@blabitalia.com

PHOSPHORESCENT CAST GLASS

Luna is a unique cast glass building material that contains a phosphorescent chemical, absorbing light during the day and glowing for hours at night. Luna is manufactured using glass recycled from car windshields and is ideal for bar fronts, tops, feature walls, flooring applications, or any interior or exterior area.

CONTENTS

Crushed glass, phosphorescent chemicals, binders

APPLICATIONS

Interior and exterior floor and wall surfaces, accent or pathway lighting, partitions, screens, fixtures, and furniture

TYPES / SIZES

Brick 7 7/8 × 3 7/8 × 2 3/8" (20 × 9.8 × 6 cm); Sheet 18 × 18" (46 × 46 cm)

ENVIRONMENTAL

A portion of the glass is recycled

LIMITATIONS

Bricks are not structural

CONTACT

Architectural Systems, Inc.
150 W. 25th Street
8th Floor
New York, NY 10001
Tel: 800-793-0224
www.archsystems.com
sales@archsystems.com

TRANSFORMATIONAL MATERIAL

OKASOLAR

GLAZING WITH INTEGRAL SUN CONTROL LOUVERS

Okasolar insulating glass is a new daylighting system without any moving components. Thanks to its direction-sensitive mirror profiles, Okasolar offers efficient direction-selective sun protection, indirect illumination (by directing light towards the ceiling), and partial through-vision. In contrast to expensive sun shade devices and maintenance-intensive external adjustable blinds, Okasolar insulated glazing units reduce glare while enhancing daylighting with fixed, integrated interlayers, which selectively introduce light based on the sun's relative angle.

CONTENTS
Glass, microstructured
louver, thermal coatings

APPLICATIONS
Daylight control

ENVIRONMENTAL
Increases energy efficiency,
reduces glare

CONTACT
Okalux GmbH
Am Jospershecklein 1
Marktheidenfeld, 97828
Germany
Tel: +49 9391 9000
www.okalux.de
info@okalux.de

PANELITE IGU

INSULATED GLASS UNIT WITH TUBULAR POLYCARBONATE CORE

Expanding on the existing technology of Insulating Glass Units, which consists of a hermetically sealed airspace between glass facings, Panelite has developed a patent-pending version that encapsulates a polycarbonate honeycomb core.

This tubular core has an aesthetic function, a programmatic function (visual privacy), and a technical function (improving thermal performance). The unit modulates light and vision, allowing light transmission while maintaining visual privacy without the need for blinds or other window treatments. The tubular nature of the honeycomb core allows for complete transparency when viewed head-on but obscures the line of site when viewed from oblique angles. The composition of the units can be adjusted to meet almost any thermal, acoustical, and wind load requirements, and has a very broad range of aesthetic options.

CONTENTS

2 layers 3/16" (.5 cm) clear tempered glass, 5/8" (1.6 cm) airspace with visual-grade Panelite tubular polycarbonate honeycomb core, anodized aluminum spacer and dual-seal of polyisobutylene and silicone (1" overall unit thickness, 2.5 cm)

APPLICATIONS

Exterior facades, sloped exterior skylights and canopies

TYPES / SIZES

Module sizes up to 4 × 10' (1.2 × 3.1 m); laminated, tempered, acid-etched, or low-e coated glass, in clear or a range of standard or custom colors; 1/4" (.6 cm) or 1/8" (.3 cm) cell honeycomb core in clear or standard colors

ENVIRONMENTAL

Recyclable components, support natural daylighting, efficient use of materials

TESTS / EXAMINATIONS

Noncombustible

LIMITATIONS

Cannot be curved

CONTACT

Panelite
3341 La Cienega Place
Los Angeles, CA 90016
Tel: 310-202-1115
www.panelite.us
info@panelite.us

PARABEAM

3D WOVEN GLASS FABRIC

Parabeam 3D glass fabric is woven out of a one hundred percent e-glass yarn and consists of two deck layers bonded together by vertical piles in a sandwich structure. These piles are woven into the deck layers in order to form an integral sandwich structure. When Parabeam is impregnated with a thermoset resin, the fabric absorbs the resin and rises to a preset height due to the inherent capillary forces of the piles.

Parabeam can be used as a positive alternative to traditional sandwich laminates based on plywood, balsa, solid laminate, honeycomb, and foam substrates. Parabeam fabrics offer excellent impregnation, resilience, and drape qualities. Parabeam can also meet rigorous fire classification standards with the use of phenolic or ATH type resins.

CONTENTS
100% glass

APPLICATIONS
Structural panels, floor and ceiling panels, ducts, bulkheads

TYPES / SIZES
.1, .2, .3, .4, .5, .6, .7, and .9"
(.3, .5, .8, 1, 1.2, 1.5, 1.8 and 2.2 cm) thickness

ENVIRONMENTAL
Low styrene emissions, high strength-to-weight ratio

CONTACT
Parabeam Industrie
Vossenbeemd 1c
Helmond, 5705 CL
The Netherlands
Tel: +31 492 591 222
www.parabeam3d.com
sales@parabeam.nl

SEMITRANSPARENT PHOTOVOLTAIC GLAZING PANEL

INTELLIGENT MATERIAL

Photovol Glass transforms any glazed surface into an environmentally sound power station and effective shading device. During the manufacturing process, a laser carves a series of fine dotted lines in the ultra-thin amorphous silicon cells encapsulated within the glass. The remaining silicon generates up to forty-four watts of electricity per square meter while allowing ten percent of visible light to be transmitted through the panel. This level of light transmission allows for visibility while protecting against excessive solar heat gain, glare, and the damaging effects of UV rays.

At one square meter framed, Photovol Glass is designed to fit a wide range of building applications such as curtain walls, eaves, skylights, etc. Its aesthetic finish and edge-mounted electrical connection system provide a crisp appearance. Photovol Glass comes standard as a laminated glass unit with junction box and MC connectors for easy installation. Custom sizes and glazing options are available.

Due to its unique uniform finish, Photovol Glass also functions as a display screen, allowing the panel to be utilized both day and night. It is also possible to harness the energy produced by the panels to power high-efficiency LED lighting, which allows for a variety of interesting design opportunities.

CONTENTS
Glass, amorphous silicon, junction box, and connectors

APPLICATIONS
Glazing, power generation

TYPES / SIZES
.4" (1 cm) thick standard glass, .5" (1.3 cm) thick strengthened glass

ENVIRONMENTAL
Renewable energy supply, mitigates solar radiation and glare

CONTACT
MSK Corporation
STEC Joho Building, 17F
1-24-1 West Shinjuku
Tokyo, 160-0023 Japan
Tel: +81 3-3342-3881
www.msk.ne.jp
staff@msk.ne.jp

RECYCLED GLASS

100% RECYCLED GLASS

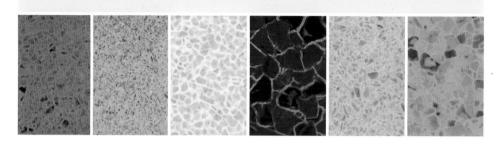

As wine consumption rises, waste glass collections improve, and landfill charges continue to increase in the UK, there is a large and growing surplus of waste green bottle glass. The Green Bottle Unit produces one hundred percent recycled glass material in response to the growing need for environmentally sound materials in the design and construction industries. This glass may be used internally and externally for paving, countertops, wall panels, and art tiles and can ultimately be recycled into future products.

GBU recycled glass products are appropriate for all kinds of construction and development projects, as they are durable enough to replace natural stone, cement and ceramics and are aesthetic rivals to granite and marble.

CONTENTS
100% recycled glass

APPLICATIONS
Tiles for interior and exterior paving, wall cladding, kitchen worktops, backsplashes

TYPES / SIZES
4 × 4 × .4–2.4" (10 × 10 × 1–6 cm) to 59 × 27.5" (150 × 70 cm)

ENVIRONMENTAL
100% recycled material from bottles, windows, and televisions

TESTS / EXAMINATIONS
British standard skid/slip, strength tests

CONTACT
Green Bottle Unit LLP
Hothouse
274 Richmond Road
London, E8 3QW UK
Tel: +00 44 (0) 207 241 7487
www.green-bottle.co.uk

SOLERA

HIGH-PERFORMANCE TRANSLUCENT GLAZING

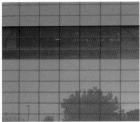

Solera is a high-performance translucent glazing made of glass. As a light diffuser, it is the equivalent of three to four layers of etched glass. Solera allows glare-free light penetration because incoming light is refracted multiple times and will bounce off ceilings and walls deep into interior spaces. It is therefore possible to reduce interior lighting loads as a result.

Solera also possesses very high thermal and acoustic insulation properties. A U-value of 0.20 BTU/s.f./hrF° gives Solera twice the insulating value of a regular double-glazed unit. An STC of 44 is about eight times as attenuating as a regular double-glazed unit.

Specified with any glass (tint, treatment, thickness) from any supplier, Solera integrates well with adjacent vision glass. Solera is ready for integration with any curtain wall, window, or skylight system.

CONTENTS
94% glass, 3% silicone, 2% aluminum, 1% acrylic

APPLICATIONS
Use adjacent to vision glass to control glare and deliver soft, diffuse daylight

TYPES / SIZES
60 × 180" (152.5 × 457 cm) maximum size

ENVIRONMENTAL
97% recyclable, optimizes energy performance by delivering deep penetration of daylight

LIMITATIONS
Curves not available

CONTACT
Advanced Glazings Ltd.
70 King's Road
PO Box 1460, Station A
Sydney, NS B1P6R7
Canada
Tel: 902-794-2899
www.advanced
glazings.com
info@advanced
glazings.com

SPHERE GLASS

DOME-SHAPED GLASS SPHERES ATTACHED TO FLAT PANELS

Sphere Glass provides a novel form for 3D glass. Hemispherical glass spheres are fused to clear or cast background glass panels. Spheres can be added to one side or both sides of the panel, and they can be cast (textured) or clear, with or without color. The spheres may be made up to two feet in diameter.

CONTENTS
100% glass

APPLICATIONS
Vertical wall partitions, backbars, sidelites, door lights, feature walls, suspended ceiling panels

TYPES / SIZES
Clear background panels up to 88 × 126" (223.5 × 320 cm), cast background panels up to 76 × 135" (193 × 343 cm). Spheres are produced in three different diameters and can be made up to 24" (61 cm) in diameter. Panels and spheres are available in clear, crystal clear, aqua blue, blue, bluegreen, green, gray, and bronze colors.

ENVIRONMENTAL
Zero-waste manufacturing process

CONTACT
Nathan Allan Glass Studios Inc.
110-12011 Riverside Way
Richmond, BC V6W 1K6
Canada
Tel: 604-277-8533 x225
www.nathanallan.com

SQUARE CHAIR NO. 5

GLASS CHAIR MADE WITH FLEXIBLE SUSPENSION SYSTEM

  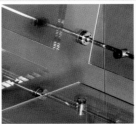 

Designed by Robert Buss, Square Chair No. 5 is a modern piece of furniture made of glass and steel, the first comfortable and flexible glass chair. This elegant, transparent construction makes use of a patented suspension system developed to increase comfort and modularity within various furniture designs. This system is comprised of four stainless steel spring rods and allows the seat and chair back to pivot in order to adjust to the load and position of the user.

CONTENTS
95% tempered glass, 4% stainless steel, 0.8% plastic, 0.2% rubber

APPLICATIONS
Interior and exterior seating

TYPES / SIZES
22.5 × 22.5 × 31"
(57 × 57 × 78 cm)

ENVIRONMENTAL
Recyclable materials

CONTACT
PUSH>
Westerkampstrasse 1
Osnabrueck, 49082
Germany
Tel: +49 (0) 541 5000 656
www.pushdesign.de

SWISSFLAM

INTUMESCENT GLAZING SYSTEM

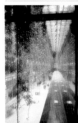

SGG Swissflam is a fire resistant and fully insulated glazing system produced from sheets of multi-laminated safety glass, separated by clear intumescent layers. In the event of a fire, the intumescent layers turn opaque and expand to form an insulating heat shield, blocking the transmission of radiated and conducted heat. The layers and seals provide an integral barrier against smoke, flames, and hot toxic gases.

CONTENTS
Glass, polysulphide sealant, alkali-silicate

APPLICATIONS
Transparent fire-rated enclosures

TYPES / SIZES
10 × 14" (25 × 35 cm) to 77 × 124" (195 × 315 cm) panel size, 1.3" (3.2 cm) thick

TESTS / EXAMINATIONS
ITS/WHI 60-minute transparent wall per ASTM E-11

CONTACT
Vetrotech Saint-Gobain
Stauffacherstrasse 128
Bern, CH-3000 Switzerland
Tel: +41 (0) 31 336 81 81
www.vetrotech.com

TAFFETA

TEXTURED-GLASS TILE SURFACING AND FLOORING

UltraGlas Taffeta features a subtle and durable embossed texture on the exposed surface. Many designs may be specified with embossed textures for a more tactile and rustic appearance or in a debossed orientation with the texture or design on the number two side, for a smoother, more "glassy" exposed surface. Dozens of standard colors may be specified and custom colors may be commissioned. Custom designs may also be commissioned.

Permanent, lead-free colorations are opaque to completely hide the setting materials used. UltraGlas colors are high-fired, fusing the color pigments into the body of the glass itself for a permanent bond. Color will not peel, separate, bubble, or react to chemicals. UltraGlas products are nonabsorbent and nonabrasive, and their impact resistance is comparable to or greater than that of ceramic tiles. Embossed UltraGlasTile is available in a comprehensive line of dozens of standard designs, including field tiles, liners, and corners.

CONTENTS
Low-iron clear glass

APPLICATIONS
Horizontal and vertical surfaces (interior and exterior), including wet environments

TYPES / SIZES
10'-6" × 6'-6" (3.2 × 2 m) maximum panel size, 5/16" (.8 cm) standard thickness; custom sizes available

ENVIRONMENTAL
May be specified in 100% recycled glass

CONTACT
UltraGlas Inc.
9200 Gazette Avenue
Chatsworth, CA 91311
Tel: 800-777-2332
www.ultraglas.com
sales@ultraglas.com

TTURA

EPOXY RESIN-BASED COMPOSITE CONTAINING RECYCLED GLASS

Ttura was developed as a result of a collaboration between Resin Building Products Limited and Sheffield Hallam University's Art and Design Research Centre, which has been at the forefront of research into open loop solutions for waste glass for a number of years.

Ttura is an attractive, highly versatile, and durable material containing eighty-five percent recycled glass, which can be used for a variety of purposes, including internal and external furniture, paving, work surfaces, flooring, and architectural cladding. The recycled glass comes from automotive, industrial, and postconsumer sources and is consolidated with a solvent-free resin binder. The material can be produced to an almost infinite color palette, using a combination of resin color and glass mix.

CONTENTS
85% recycled glass, 15% solvent-free epoxy resin

ENVIRONMENTAL
Recycled material, solvent-free resin binder

APPLICATIONS
Flooring, paving, tiles, cladding, work surfaces, counter tops, furniture, architectural features

CONTACT
Resin Building Products Limited
Unit 7, Plumb Estate
Sandall Stones Road
Doncaster, DN3 1QR UK
Tel: +01302 881394
www.ttura.com
ttura@resbuild.co.uk

GLASS FLOORING AND SURFACES

UltraGlas Inc. offers an embossed low-iron glass for flooring and other surface applications. UltraGlasFlooring may be laminated for suspended applications. It is available in seventeen standard surface textures that satisfy coefficient of friction requirements for dry environments; the application of a non-slip coating is recommended for wet environments.

UltraGlasFlooring is available in opaque or translucent versions as well as dozens of colors and patterns. Custom colors may also be specified. UltraGlas leadfree monolithic colors are "high-fired," fusing the color pigments into the body of the glass itself for a permanent bond; color will therefore not peel, separate, bubble, or react to chemicals. UltraGlas products are nonabsorbent and nonabrasive, and their impact resistance is comparable to or greater than that of ceramic tiles. Maintenance is comparable to any glass surface.

CONTENTS
Low-iron glass

APPLICATIONS
Horizontal and vertical
surfaces

TYPES / SIZES
10'-6" × 6'-6" (3.2 × 2 m)
maximum panel size, 3/8–
3/4" (1–2 cm) thick, laminated or unlaminated

ENVIRONMENTAL
100% recycled glass may
be specified

CONTACT
UltraGlas Inc.
9200 Gazette Avenue
Chatsworth, CA 91311
Tel: 800-777-2332
www.ultraglas.com
sales@ultraglas.com

ULTRAPERFORMING MATERIAL

VANCEVA

METALLIC INTERLAYERS FOR LAMINATED GLASS

Vanceva metallic interlayers are permanently bonded between two sheets of glass to form durable, high performance glazing. The Vanceva metallic interlayers are available in three distinct textures that reflect and scatter light for dramatic visual effect. The interlayers are made with heat- and light-stable pigments that resist fading.

Laminated glass with Vanceva assures durability, ease of maintenance, and protection against corrosion. Vanceva interlayers reduce solar radiation, exterior noise, and damage from potential impact.

CONTENTS
Polyvinyl butyral (PVB)
films

APPLICATIONS
Exterior and interior glazing

TYPES / SIZES
144 × 78" (366 × 198 cm)
maximum size, designed for
standard glass thicknesses

ENVIRONMENTAL
Solar radiation protection,
acoustic performance

TESTS / EXAMINATIONS
ASTM F1233, UL972,
CPSC Cat II

CONTACT
Solutia Inc.
575 Maryville Centre Drive
St. Louis, MO 63141
Tel: 877-674-1233
www.vanceva.com
glazin@solutia.com

WATERGLASS

CAST GLASS WITH ENCASED BUBBLE EFFECT

Waterglass from Architectural Systems, Inc., is made from crushed glass and proprietary chemicals, which capture air bubbles within the material. Waterglass is available in brick and sheet forms and is ideal for bar fronts, countertops, feature walls, ceilings, and column covers in interior or exterior environments.

CONTENTS
Glass, air-entraining chemicals

APPLICATIONS
Interior wall surfaces, partitions, screens, fixtures, and furniture

TYPES / SIZES
36 × 36" (91.5 × 91.5 cm) sheet

ENVIRONMENTAL
Portion of glass has recycled content

LIMITATIONS
Not structural, material not recommended for flooring

CONTACT
Architectural Systems, Inc.
150 W. 25th Street, 8th Fl.
New York, NY 10001
Tel: 800-793-0224
www.archsystems.com
sales@archsystems.com

07: **PAINT + PAPER**

LOTUSAN

WATER-REPELLENT PAINT

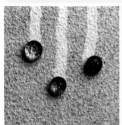 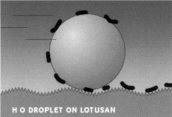 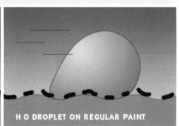

H O DROPLET ON LOTUSAN

H O DROPLET ON REGULAR PAINT

The leaves of the lotus plant are immaculately clean after every rainfall because dirt and microorganisms are unable to obtain a hold on the microstructured, non-wettable surfaces of the leaves. Dirt particles, algae, and fungal spores do not become firmly attached to the leaves, merely lying loosely on the surfaces. Rain simply washes the particles away.

A team of scientists under Dr. Wilhelm Barthlott at the University of Bonn discovered the so-called "lotus effect" by learning from nature's model. The Lotusan facade paint is the first successful practical application of the lotus effect, and about four million square meters of facade surfacing have since been coated with Lotusan paint.

CONTENTS
Paint with water-repellent
microstructure

APPLICATIONS
Exterior surfaces

ENVIRONMENTAL
No cleaners or chemicals
needed

LIMITATIONS
For exterior use only

CONTACT
Sto AG
Ehrnebachstr. 1
Stühlingen, 79780
Germany
Tel: +1 404 3463666
www.sto.de
marketingsupport@
stocorp.com

REVERSACOL

PHOTOCHROMIC DYE

James Robinson is a world leader in the development of innovative photochromic dyes. Reversacol is a special dye that reversibly changes color upon exposure to ultraviolet sources, such as sunlight. Reversacol photochromic dyes are offered in twenty vibrant colors. There is also a range of unique single-molecule photochromic grays, which offer the advantage of achieving a neutral color without the need to mix several dyes.

Reversacol can be added to plastics, inks and coatings, and applications including, but not limited to, ophthalmic photochromic lenses and sunglasses, security inks and coatings for passports and brand protection, perfume and cosmetic packaging, optical switches, mobile phone covers, ski and sportswear, and nail varnish.

Reversacol photochromics can be combined with a wide range of special-effect colorants, such as light angle–dependent interference pigments, thermochromics, liquid crystals, and permanent dyes to produce unusual photochromic effects.

CONTENTS
Photochromic dye

APPLICATIONS
Interior panels, lenses, security coatings, cosmetics, accessories, art

TYPES / SIZES
20 colors available

ENVIRONMENTAL
Reduces solar radiation

LIMITATIONS
Not for exterior use

CONTACT
James Robinson Ltd.
PO Box B3, Hillhouse Lane
Huddersfield
West Yorkshire, HD1 6BU
UK
Tel: +44 (0)1484 320500
www.james-robinson.ltd.uk
sales@james-robinson.ltd.uk

UV/FX

ULTRAVIOLET LIGHT-ACTIVATED SCENERY

UV/FX Scenic Productions has developed a process for intermixing fluorescent paints to achieve a wide spectrum of colors when exposed to ultraviolet light. UV/FX designs and paints day-to-night scenery, single image scenery, dual image scenery, complete invisible scenery, and 3D scenery for theatrical sets and art installations on most surfaces.

CONTENTS
UV responsive paint, flame-retardant muslin fabric, light

APPLICATIONS
Theatrical backdrops, point of purchase displays, art walls, floors, and ceilings

LIMITATIONS
Exterior use limited to one year

CONTACT
UV/FX Scenic Productions
171 Pier Avenue
Santa Monica, CA 90405
Tel: 310-821-2657
www.uvfx.com

3D WALLPAPER

TEXTILE WALLPAPER

London-based Tracy Kendall has liberated wallpaper from flatland. Her handcrafted, handsewn fabrications consist of cut and layered papers, polyester thread, and applied sequins. The result is walls that seem to breathe, dance, and crackle, thus stimulating the senses. Tracy Kendall has developed at least three types of wallpaper: In the White Room, Cut, and Sequin.

In the White Room is designed to add depth and texture to a wall and is made of paper and thread; Cut is a handcut wallpaper, which can be used either on its own or with a patterned or colored paper beneath it to reveal the cut sections; and Sequin comes alive when lit, as the sequins project their own patterns onto other walls and surfaces.

CONTENTS
Wallpaper, polyester thread, sequins

APPLICATIONS
Wall surfacing, art

TYPES / SIZES
In the White Room, Cut, Sequin

LIMITATIONS
Interior walls only, not fire rated

CONTACT
Tracy Kendall
401 Wandsworth Road
London, SW8 2JP UK
Tel: +00 44 (0) 20 7640 9071
www.tracykendall.com
info@tracykendall.com

PAPER SOFTWALL

EXPANDABLE PAPER AND WOOL ROOM PARTITION

The Paper Softwall is a lightweight freestanding wall that can be arranged into almost any shape or easily compressed into a compact sheaf and stored away. Softwall dampens sound and can both absorb and transmit light. The product is made from four hundred layers of honeycombed translucent white, fire-retardant paper, bounded by natural wool felt ends. The thick felt ends fold to create handles when the wall is open, and form a casing when the wall is compressed.

The Paper Softwall is modular, as the felt ends have Velcro fasteners, which can link walls together. Although paper is delicate, the Paper Softwall's honeycomb design makes it surprisingly resilient to normal handling.

CONTENTS
Flame-retardant paper, wool felt

APPLICATIONS
Acoustic control, space divider, exhibit booth, feature wall

TYPES / SIZES
46" (117 cm) and 78" (198 cm) tall versions, each expandable from 2" to 25' (5 cm to 7.6 m)

ENVIRONMENTAL
Low embodied energy, recyclable, natural materials

LIMITATIONS
Not yet for exterior use

CONTACT
Molo
206 - 869 Beatty Street
Vancouver, BC V6B 2M6
Canada
Tel: 604-696-2501
www.molodesign.com
info@molodesign.com

MONOPLANAR PAPER CHAIR

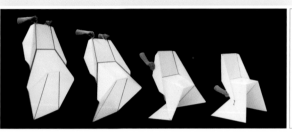

Papton is a lightweight chair that emerges like origami from a folded composite panel. For their design of the chair, Fuchs + Funke sought to obtain maximum stability with minimum weight as well as unlimited functionality and sculptural form. The chair is therefore the result of a simple polygonal pattern, which conveys a clear, monoplanar quality.

Papton's structure is based on subdividing panels into load-bearing areas and bending zones, and the partial removal of the top layer on one side allows for controlled folding. Low weight and volume ensure a dense package of unfolded chairs (up to eighty chairs fit on a standard Euro pallet).

CONTENTS
Cardboard honeycomb panels (other composite panels available)

APPLICATIONS
Seating

TYPES / SIZES
31.5 × 24.5 × 21"
(80 × 62 × 53 cm)

CONTACT
Fuchs + Funke
Schwedter Str. 34a
Berlin, 10435
Germany
Tel: +49 30 44047952
www.fuchs-funke.de
info@fuchs-funke.de

ULTRAPERFORMING PRODUCT

PINNACLE

N° 101123-002

RECYCLED-PAPER PANEL WITH SANDED FINISH

PINnacle is a recycled-paper panel supplied with a velvetlike sanded surface for a more elegant appearance than conventional tackboards. Both PINnacle 440 and Class A fire-rated PINnacle NCFR panels may be used as a pin-up surface, acoustic treatment, or prefinished wall covering. The panels are easy to maintain, and their uniform thickness makes them a good substrate for fabric wrapping.

CONTENTS
Paper (65–98% recycled postconsumer content)

APPLICATIONS
Prefinished wall covering, tackboards, acoustic treatment for interior vertical surfaces and ceilings

TYPES / SIZES
4 × 8' (1.2 × 2.4 m) panels, 3/8" (1 cm) or 1/2" (1.3 cm) thick; 440 and NCFR versions

ENVIRONMENTAL
High recycled content, low embodied energy

TESTS / EXAMINATIONS
440 Homasote: UL listing R16381, ASTM E-84 Flame Spread Class C
NCFR Homasote: UL listings R5268, 91G7; ASTM E-84 Flame Spread Class A

LIMITATIONS
Vertical installation only, not for exterior use

CONTACT
Homasote
932 Lower Ferry Road
West Trenton, NJ 08628
Tel: 800-257-9491
www.homasote.com
sales@homasote.com

NATURAL FIBER COMPOSITE BOARD

Richlite panels are extremely dense, strong, and stable and are made of layered craft paper (or abacca fibers in the case of Richlite Hemp). The material was originally developed for the aerospace industry as tooling, the marine industry as fiberglass reinforcement, and most recently the action sports industry for outdoor skate ramp surfaces.

Richlite resists scratching, staining, and heat damage and will not harbor bacteria or pests. Richlite's color is integral throughout the material, and its natural appearance develops a deep patina over time and with use.

Inherent strength and stability makes Richlite a popular choice in finishes for architectural use. Extreme cantilevers and long spans can be created without the requirement of designing extra support. Thermal contraction and expansion is minimal, and therefore need not be a design consideration.

Made with the most environmentally benign production methods and materials currently available, the paper or abacca fiber used for Richlite comes from certified or renewable resources, respectively, and the resin is harvested locally. During the saturation and drying process, over ninety-nine percent of the volatile organic compounds are incinerated. The heat from this incineration process is used for the drying process to optimize energy use and minimize thermal pollution. There is no hazardous waste generated in the process.

CONTENTS
70% paper (or abacca fiber), 30% phenolic resin

APPLICATIONS
Counters, architectural millwork, interior wall panels, stair treads and risers, exterior siding, cutting boards

TYPES / SIZES
1/4" (.6 cm) and 1/2" (1.3 cm) sheets up to 5 × 12' (1.5 × 3.7 m), 3/4–3" (1.9–7.5 cm)-thick counters

ENVIRONMENTAL
Low VOCs, wood pulp from FSC sources (Richlite), rapidly renewable abacca fibers (Richlite Hemp)

TESTS / EXAMINATIONS
ASTM E84, EPA 7000, UL Building Materials (BHWV) Hardboard

CONTACT
Rainier Richlite Corporation
624 East 15th Street
Tacoma, WA 98421
Tel: 888-383-5533
www.richlite.com
info@richlite.com

SQUAK MOUNTAIN STONE

LIGHTWEIGHT RECYCLED-PAPER–CEMENT COMPOSITE

Squak Mountain Stone is a paper and cement-based composite developed by Ameé Quiriconi as a solution for reusing waste paper. Its proprietary composition makes Squak Mountain Stone lighter than concrete and stone, and it eliminates the need for rebar or other reinforcing steel. The result is a product that is relatively easy to ship, handle, and install.

Visually, Squak Mountain Stone appears to have the depth and characteristics of natural stone. Veins of mineral deposits can be seen meandering through the material, while the texture looks as if it's created by metamorphic processes rather than by man-made means. Squak Mountain Stone is also offered in many different colors.

"Selecting materials is an emotional action. We want the products to not only match our values of environmental and social responsibility but also be beautiful and cost effective" says Quiriconi. "When I watch people slowly stroke the tops of our slabs, I know we've been able to capture it all in Squak Mountain Stone."

CONTENTS
Mixed waste paper, Portland cement, fly ash, crushed granite and/or crushed glass, iron oxide pigments

APPLICATIONS
Precast countertops, tiles, tabletops, decorative bowls, custom sculptural sinks

TYPES / SIZES
Countertops: 25.5 × 72" (65 × 183 cm) or 30 × 48" (76 × 122 cm); Tabletops: 18 × 18" (45.5 × 45.5 cm), 24 × 24" (61 × 61 cm), 30 × 30" (76 × 76 cm), 36 × 36" (91.5 × 91.5 cm) Custom sizes available

ENVIRONMENTAL
All raw materials except cement are recycled, low embodied-energy manufacturing process, local material for Pacific Northwest projects

TESTS / EXAMINATIONS
ASTM C109 (Compressive strength), ASTM C880 (Flexural Strength), ASTM C648-04 (Breaking Strength for tiles), ANSI Z124.3, Section 5.2/5.5 (Stain/Chemical Resistance), ASTM C97 (Absorption), ASTM C856 (Petrographic Examination)

LIMITATIONS
Not for exterior use; like natural stones, product may develop stains

CONTACT
Tiger Mountain Innovations, Inc.
16130 Woodinville-Redmond Road NE, Suite #1
Woodinville, WA 98072
Tel: 800-281-9785
www.squakmountain stone.com

3D RECYCLED WALLPAPER

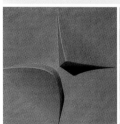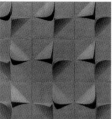

V2 tiles are 3D, reconfigurable, inexpensive wallpaper tiles that allow one to customize the feel, look, and acoustic properties of any environment in minutes. V2 wallpaper is made from one hundred percent pre- and post-consumer waste paper that is molded in a thermoforming process. Production of the tiles takes place in a closed loop manufacturing environment where paper and water are continually cycled through the process, virtually eliminating waste. The tiles are also completely recyclable at the end of their useful life.

Different patterns may be achieved by rotating the tiles, allowing users to have unique patterned wallpaper in wall and ceiling areas. The tiles can be installed temporarily with double stick tape, thumb tacks, staples, nails, etc. or permanently with water-based wallpaper pastes. The product can be painted or finished in a variety of ways, including standard paints, magic markers, and bio-benign varnishes. In addition, the tiles may be easily cut to fit light switches and other fixtures with scissors or a utility knife.

CONTENTS
100% recycled waste paper

APPLICATIONS
Aesthetic and acoustic treatment for interior surfaces

TYPES / SIZES
12 × 12 × 2.25"
(30.5 × 30.5 × 5.7 cm) tiles

ENVIRONMENTAL
100% pre-and post-consumer recycled waste paper, closed-loop manufacturing process, recyclable

TESTS / EXAMINATIONS
ASTM E84 Pending

LIMITATIONS
Not for exterior use, tiles may be damaged with high impact

CONTACT
Mio
340 North 12th Street
Unit 301
Philadelphia, PA 19107
Tel: 215-925-9359
www.mioculture.com
info@mioculture.com

MULTIDIMENSIONAL MATERIAL

YUM!

SCRATCH-AND-SNIFF WALLPAPER

Developed by Alex Schweder and Dieter Janssen and manufactured by the Stinehour Press, YUM! is a scratch-and-sniff wallpaper that smells faintly of fresh bread. The artists developed the wallpaper for a gallery installation, seeking to explore the relationship between color and scent with the goal of creating a "succulent" space. Alex and Dieter designed three sheets with the same striped pattern but with different ratios of scented scratch-and-sniff varnishes and colored inks. The resulting effect is the creation of a space with varying degrees of visual and olfactory intensity based on one's proximity to the different sheets.

CONTENTS
Paper, scented varnishes, colored inks

APPLICATIONS
Interior finishes

TYPES / SIZES
21.5 × 34" (54.5 × 86.5 cm)

LIMITATIONS
No coating to protect against water damage

CONTACT
The Stinehour Press
853 Lancaster Road
Lunenburg, VT 05906
Toll-free: 1-800-331-7753
www.stinehourpress.com

08: **FABRIC**

AIRTECTURE

AIR-INFLATED FABRIC STRUCTURES

Building with air, the most natural of all materials, is a special challenge because air-inflated components are used in place of the usual load-bearing components.

The idea behind Airtecture is based on mechanically pre-tensioned membrane constructions that have been used for several interesting buildings (e.g. the German Pavilion at the EXPO 1992 in Seville, Spain, or the Denver International Airport in Colorado). The most important innovation of Airtecture is that the membranes are not mechanically pre-tensioned but by means of air pressure in such a way that they are able to bear loads.

German pneumatic experts Festo modelled Airtecture after early air-supported structures. In contrast to such buildings, however, Airtecture works with a much higher air pressure and also has atmospheric pressure in the inside.

CONTENTS
Vitroflex (natural rubber and integrated glass fiber fabric), polyester, polyamid, hostaflon, pneumatic muscles, steel rails

APPLICATIONS
Lightweight structures

TYPES / SIZES
Varies

ENVIRONMENTAL
Efficient use of material

LIMITATIONS
Can withstand a snow load of up to 10 lbs/ft^2 (50 kg/m^2) and a wind speed of up to 50 mph (80 km/h)

CONTACT
Festo AG
PO Box 73726
Esslingen, D-73728
Germany
Tel: +49 711 347-3880
www.festo.com

CARBON FIBER FABRIC

HIGH-STRENGTH CLOTH WOVEN FROM CARBON FIBER

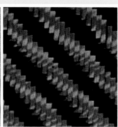

When advanced composite technology was first introduced in the early 1960s, the emphasis was on increased performance by means of reducing structural weight. When carbon fiber was developed in the late 1960s, it revolutionized applications demanding light weight and high strength.

Moreover, carbon fiber's extremely small diameter (6 to 10 microns) allowed a bending radius of less than 1/16"; traditional high-strength steel could be used instead of diamond-tip tools for cutting, trimming, drilling, and machining; and carbon fiber became available in a variety of strengths, stiffnesses, and other mechanical properties.

The introduction of carbon fibers radically influenced the design of aircraft, racing vehicles, sports equipment, and other lightweight structures, and the material continues to be utilized in new applications today.

CONTENTS
100% carbon fiber

APPLICATIONS
Strong, lightweight
structures

TYPES / SIZES
0.012–0.016" (.03–.04 cm)
thick

ENVIRONMENTAL
High strength-to-weight
ratio

CONTACT
Fibre Glast
95 Mosier Parkway
Brookville, OH 45309
Tel: 800-330-6368
www.fibreglast.com
customerservice@
fibreglast.com

CIRCULATION

MULTIDIMENSIONAL WOOL RUG AND WALL SURFACE

Designed by Monika Piatkowski, the Circulation rug and wall surface is comprised of circular wool felt pellets set within a honeycomb structure. This simple configuration allows the surface to be smooth and resilient while simultaneously being soft and comfortable.

Circulation is edged with Hessian webbing but other materials can be commissioned. The rug and pellet size may also be commissioned to custom dimensions.

CONTENTS
100% wool felt

APPLICATIONS
Floor rug or wall covering; may be used as an acoustic treatment for interiors

TYPES / SIZES
Made to order; pellet size pictured .8 × 1" (2 × 2.5 cm)

ENVIRONMENTAL
Rapidly renewable natural material

LIMITATIONS
Not for external use or for high-traffic interiors

CONTACT
Hive
Unit 1.02 Oxo Tower Wharf
Bargehouse Street
London, SE1 9PH UK
Tel: +44 (0) 2072 619 791
www.hivespace.com
hive@hivespace.com

TOPOGRAPHIC WOOL RUG AND WALL COVERING

Designed by Monika Piatkowski, Cityscape elevates the notion of conventional loop pile and knotted rugs to a new dimension, moving away from thread material to a dense flat medium. In its utilization of multiple layers like an architectural contour model, Cityscape creates visual interest without requiring the application of conventional 2D patterns, multiple textures, or varied materials.

CONTENTS
100% wool felt

APPLICATIONS
Floor rug or wall covering; may be used as an acoustic treatment for interiors

TYPES / SIZES
Made to order; maximum width 71" (180 cm)

ENVIRONMENTAL
Rapidly renewable natural material

LIMITATIONS
Not for external use or for high-traffic interiors

CONTACT
Hive
Unit 1.02 Oxo Tower Wharf
Bargehouse Street
London, SE1 9PH UK
Tel: +44 (0) 2072 619 791
www.hivespace.com
hive@hivespace.com

MULTIDIMENSIONAL PRODUCT

DIGITAL DAWN

N° 122400-001

ELECTROLUMINESCENT WINDOW COVERING

    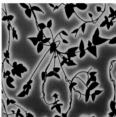

Designed by Rachel Wingfield, Digital Dawn is a textile that responds to environmental stimuli. It functions as a traditional window blind with a reactive surface that is in constant flux, growing in luminosity in response to its surroundings.

Wingfield intended Digital Dawn to emulate the process of photosynthesis using electroluminescent printing technology. Light-dependent sensors monitor the changing light levels within a space, triggering the growth of the organic foliage on the blind. A natural environment will appear to grow on the window surface, showing changing light levels within a space can have profound and physiological impact on our sense of well-being.

CONTENTS
Silk, electroluminescence, electronics

APPLICATIONS
Light, window blind

TYPES / SIZES
25 × 51" (64 × 130 cm), custom sizes available

LIMITATIONS
Not for exterior use

CONTACT
Loop.pH Ltd & Elumin8
11 Springfield House,
5 Tyssen Street
London, E8 2LY UK
Tel: +44 (0)7792474091
www.loop.ph
loop@loop.ph

DIGITAL NATURE

DIGITALLY DESIGNED WALLCOVERING

Exploring new ways to reference patterning found in nature, Karim Rashid digitally generated five designs and manipulated them to resemble multiple plant, animal, land, and human anatomies. The five patterns in the Digital Nature collection are available in chartreuse, cyan, magenta, silver, and sixty-five other colors, allowing different iterations.

The designs are: Replicant—a large-scale vertical wire frame pattern that resembles successive joints of an x-rayed leg structure or strong plant stalks that "climb" the height of the wall; Flexous —a pattern that creates topography on walls by referencing a molded wire frame, screen, or wrinkled fabric, which becomes luminous when the line work is lighter than its background; Zenith— zoomorphic masses of vertical strings that rise the height of the wall; Space Warp—avian-influenced patterns superposed with an irregular grid in translucent inks to reveal underprinting; and Rosetta—pairs of bud-like, spiralized forms composed across the wall surface in a serialized design.

CONTENTS
Vinyl

APPLICATIONS
Wallcovering for interior
vertical surfaces

TYPES / SIZES
54" (137 cm) wide; sold by
the yard

TESTS / EXAMINATIONS
ASTM E-84, MEA approved,
Class A fire rated

LIMITATIONS
Not for external use

CONTACT
Wolf-Gordon
33-00 47th Avenue
Long Island City, NY 11101
Tel: 800-347-0550
www.wolf-gordon.com
info@wolf-gordon.com

FABRILED

LED SIGNAGE WOVEN INTO FLEXIBLE FABRIC

FabriLED consists of LED-based electronics woven into cotton fabric. It is flexible, lightweight, and fully programmable. Invented by Sarnoff (the old RCA labs), FabriLED may be wall- or ceiling-hung, mounted in windows, or wrapped around corners. The product includes software, which provides a variety of data-scrolling capabilities.

CONTENTS
Cotton, electronic circuit board

APPLICATIONS
Point-of-purchase displays, signage, message boards

TYPES / SIZES
5 character sign: 4–5' (1.2–1.5 m); 8 character sign: 7–8' (2.1–2.4 m); custom sizes available

ENVIRONMENTAL
LEDs are very efficient and long-lasting; efficient use of materials for signage; low transportation costs

LIMITATIONS
Current versions not weatherproof

CONTACT
FabriLED, LLC
4949 Greenbrooke Drive
Southeast Kentwood, MI 49512
Tel: 616-698-0781
www.fabriled.com

FUZZY LIGHT SWITCH

FUZZY CAPACITIVE LIGHT SENSOR

International Fashion Machines (IFM) provides private research and consulting in electronic textiles to a variety of clients, industries, and the military. They work with the latest electronic yarns and a variety of textile processes including embroidery, sewing, weaving, and braiding. IFM also creates electronic textile connections, both intra-textile and between traditional electronics and textiles.

Designed by Maggie Orth, IFM's Fuzzy Light Switches are woven and embroidered touch sensors for dimming lights or controlling electronic devices with the touch of a hand. IFM's interactive textiles can cover a wall, control the lights in the room, or become part of the furniture.

CONTENTS
Polyester, wool, and nylon fabric, rayon yarns, conductive yarns

APPLICATIONS
Interior lighting control

TYPES / SIZES
Standard wall plate dimensions: 2.75 × 4.5" (7 × 11.5 cm)

CONTACT
International Fashion Machines
1205 East Pike Street
Suite 2G
Seattle, WA 98112
Tel: 206-860-5166
www.ifmachines.com
info@ifmachines.com

GIVE BACK CURTAIN

FABRIC WOVEN WITH LUMINOUS PHOSPHORS

   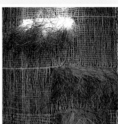

The Give Back Curtain is part of a series of techno-fabric designs that rethink the traditional and modern applications of portable fabric screens. The Give Back Curtain gives a pliable fabric matrix the capacity to illuminate, define space dynamically over time, and provide a portable form of privacy without partitions.

The Give Back Curtain recycles light through a fabrication process that integrates photo-luminescent pigments in synthetic or natural fibers. Light of a shorter wavelength, such as sunlight or fluorescent light, is absorbed by the fabric, retained, and then released as visible light emitted within another part of the color spectrum.

CONTENTS
Cotton, polymer with optical treatments

APPLICATIONS
Energy harvesting curtains, luminous privacy enclosures

ENVIRONMENTAL
Zero power consumption

CONTACT
Sheila Kennedy with
Sheetal Khanna-Ravitch
160 North Washington
Street, 8/F
Boston, MA 02114
Tel: 617-367-3784
www.kvarch.net

HOLOFIBER

RESPONSIVE POLYESTER-BASED TEXTILE

Utilizing cutting-edge nanotechnology, Hologenix has found a way to introduce millions of microscopic lenses permanently into natural and synthetic textiles. Holofiber fabric works with the body's own energy, modifying the spectrum of visible and invisible light and recycling energy back into the body. Holofiber actually builds strength, improves circulation, and accelerates muscle recovery. With increased oxygen, muscles work better, recover faster, and avoid painful cramping. Holofiber is completely safe and is designed to be permanently effective.

CONTENTS
100% polyester or blends with other natural and synthetic textiles including cotton, wool, rayon, nylon, acrylic, spandex, etc.

APPLICATIONS
Apparel, hosiery, medical and performance wraps, gloves, equestrian products, footwear, sleep pads

TYPES / SIZES
Spun fiber, spun yarns, textured filament yarns, bi-component staple yarn

TESTS / EXAMINATIONS
Two blind clinical studies have proven product efficacy

CONTACT
Hologenix LLC
PO Box 1649
Fort Mill, SC 29716
Tel: 866-822-4700
www.holofiber.com
info@holofiber.com

JELARA

BI-ELASTIC FABRIC KNITTED WITH TEFLON AND POLYESTER

Jens J. Meyer is a freelance artist who has worked with fabric sculptures and installations since 1992. Highly bi-elastic textiles enable 3D forming of fabric elements and the realization of sculptural ideas.

Seeking a more durable elastic fabric, Jens collaborated with the ITV textile research institute to combine the UV-resistant qualities of the Teflon-based yarn Tenara (by W. L. Gore) with a new, highly elastic yarn that contains no polyurethane (it degrades in UV light).

Jens succeeded in June 2004 in developing the first test sample of Jelara, and he is now working on production of the material.

CONTENTS
65% PTFE Tenara (by W. L. Gore), 35% polyester

APPLICATIONS
Fabric sculptures and installations, mobile fabric lightweight constructions, textile design objects

TYPES / SIZES
Width 3 or 6' (0.9 or 1.8 m), .06 lbs/ft^2 (300g/m^2)

CONTACT
Jens J. Meyer
Bonifaciusring 14
Essen, D-45309
Germany
Tel: +49 (0) 201558211
www.jj-meyer.com
info@jj-meyer.de

KRYSTAL WEAVE

TRANSLUCENT POLYMER FABRIC

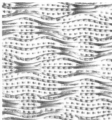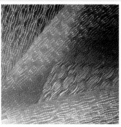

Libby Kowalski of Kova Textiles developed the Krystal Weave collection because she was inspired by the water-clear yarn that is used prominently as the horizontal element in the fabric. A glistening matrix of transparent and translucent threads, Krystal Weave fabric is like a crystalline curtain, which offers a variety of possibilities for dividing spaces, enhancing windows, and covering uphol-stered wall panels in commercial and residential spaces.

CONTENTS
85% polymer, 10% nylon, 5% polyester

APPLICATIONS
Flat window panels, room dividers, decorative screens, theatrical backdrops

TYPES / SIZES
54" (137 cm) wide

ENVIRONMENTAL
Polymer yarns contain recycled content

LIMITATIONS
Fabrics are heavy and do not fold or pleat easily

CONTACT
Kova Textiles, LLC
32 Union Square East
Suite 216
New York, NY 10003
Tel: 212-254-7591
www.kovatextiles.com
info@kovatextiles.com

LIGHTTEX

FABRIC LIGHT-CONTROL PANELS

When used as a window and skylight covering, the polyester-based Lighttex panel blocks and re-distributes direct sunlight more effectively than vertical or horizontal blinds and creates diffused interior daylight with improved uniformity.

Lighttex walls and space partitions enable daylight penetration while providing a view for occupants in an interior space. At an angle, the wall appears opaque, creating a sense of privacy, and yet when viewing the material directly it becomes transparent, creating a sense of openness and a view outside.

Lighttex is an integration of architecture and space, enabling architects to design flat and curved ceilings that appear as a luminous floating element in the space while providing soft light distribution. Various dramatic lighting effects can be achieved depending on the placement and type of light fixtures, creating a broad palette of solutions with simple variables.

CONTENTS
Polyester, PVC

APPLICATIONS
Daylight control in modular walls, curved and flat modular ceiling panels, window and skylight coverings

TYPES / SIZES
6 × 6' (1.8 × 1.8 m) modular panels with optional cell sizes

ENVIRONMENTAL
Increased energy savings, reduced glare for building occupants

LIMITATIONS
Not yet for exterior use

CONTACT
Lighttex Canada, Inc.
9513-56 Avenue
Edmonton, AB T6E 0B2
Canada
Tel: 800-417-7431
www.lighttex.com
sales@lighttex.com

MUTE ROOM

MEMORY FOAM-BASED ENVIRONMENT

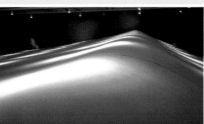

NASA invented Memory Foam over three decades ago in order to provide comfortable seating for astronauts who had to endure steep gravitational forces and spend days sitting in tight quarters. As its name suggests, the soft material conforms to the body of its user and leaves a temporary registration of this interaction.

Although the material failed in space due to its temperature sensitivity, Memory Foam has been adopted for a wide variety of consumer products including mattresses and office chairs.

Thom Faulders of Beige Design recently used Memory Foam to create his Mute Room, which was installed as a temporary listening environment for experimental electronic music at the CCA Wattis Institute in San Francisco.

CONTENTS
Memory foam, polyester foam

APPLICATIONS
Mattresses, chairs, bicycle seats

LIMITATIONS
Less effective in cold temperatures

CONTACT
Beige Design
1025 Carleton Street #14
Berkeley, CA 94710
Tel: 510-666-0892
www.beigedesign.com

MULTIDIMENSIONAL MATERIAL

DOUBLE-FACED FELT

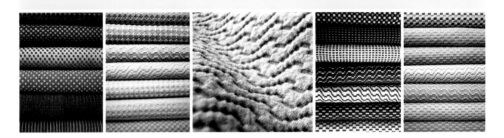

By combining decorating fabric and a laminating material, Gudlin & Grabowicz created a lively 3D felt, which can be readily processed for upholstery, clothing, and decorating. The materials used in Profil seem to be glued together, but the double-faced felt is actually mechanically adhered without the use of any chemicals.

CONTENTS
50% wool, 50% polyester

APPLICATIONS
Decorative fabric, uphol-stery, clothing

TYPES / SIZES
47" (120 cm) maximum width

ENVIRONMENTAL
No use of chemicals

CONTACT
Gudlin & Grabowicz
Laffertstrasse 3
Braunschweig, 38118
Germany
g.zsofi@gmx.de

DATA-LAYERED SEATING TEXTILE

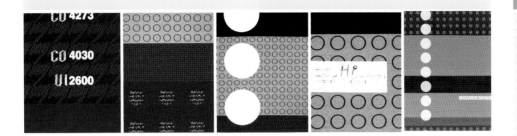

Maharam approached Hella Jongerius in 2001 with an open objective: to create a single textile that would permit a suite of chairs around a table to be cousins, each unique but all related. Jongerius's design vocabulary, playing on the concept of random order, personalization of industrial processes, and manipulation of traditional manufacturing methods and materials, lent itself ideally to this concept.

Using archetypal motifs drawn from the archives of a Swiss textile mill, Repeat is comprised of a series of patterns of a singular theme that seamlessly flow into one another over a course of several yards. Repeat Classic is a ribbon of traditional Jacquard patterns, while Repeat Dot unfurls into a modernist sequence of varied circular forms. In Repeat Classic Print and Repeat Dot Print, Jongerius embellishes further, celebrating the industrial vocabulary of the weaving process through a layer of technical nomenclature in white lacquer overprint.

Through the unexpected use of pattern and exaggerated scale, Repeat creates random order as fabric meets furniture with a predictable yet uncertain result.

CONTENTS
50–55% cotton, 24–26% polyester, 21–24% rayon, all woven on a Jacquard loom

APPLICATIONS
Seating

TYPES / SIZES
55" (140 cm) wide; repeat lengths: Classic: 123" (312.5 cm), Classic Print: 122" (310 cm), Dot: 87" (221 cm), Dot Print: 86" (218.5 cm)

TESTS / EXAMINATIONS
Classic, Classic Print: 30,000+ double rubs (Wyzenbeek Test)
Dot, Dot Print: 100,000+ double rubs (Wyzenbeek Test)

LIMITATIONS
Only recommended for seating

CONTACT
Maharam
251 Park Avenue South
New York, NY 10010
Tel: 212-614-2918
www.maharam.com

INTERFACIAL MATERIAL

STOMATEX

BREATHABLE NEOPRENE FABRIC

Neoprene is used extensively in the water sports, soft orthopedic, sportswear, footwear, equestrian, and thermal protective equipment sectors. However, conventional neoprene causes serious discomfort when worn against the skin of humans or animals. Stomatex overcomes this discomfort by dynamically removing moisture.

Stomatex embodies technology that allows impermeable materials (closed cell foams) to transfer heat and perspiration from the body. Stomatex technology has been successfully applied to closed cell neoprene with further variants under development. The product is currently being used in sports supports, equestrian products, and other similar products.

CONTENTS
Neoprene, nylon, polyester, other materials

APPLICATIONS
Thermal insulation
with moisture removal
capabilities

TYPES / SIZES
3.9 × 6.7' (1.2 × 2.05 m)
sheet size;
.08–.24" (.2–.6 cm) gauge

TESTS / EXAMINATIONS
Tested by the Institute of
Naval Medicine, The Cord
Group Ltd., Shei Chung
Industrial Co., and Under-
writers Laboratories

LIMITATIONS
Not for domestic
furnishings

CONTACT
Stomatex
Treasure House
19-21 Hatton Garden
London, EC1N 8LF UK
Tel: +44 (0) 1579 362566
www.stomatex.com
info@stomatex.com

NATURAL COTTON-FIBER INSULATION

Bonded Logic, Inc., makes insulation out of recycled blue jeans. UltraTouch is a Class-A building material made from postindustrial recycled natural cotton/denim fibers that are treated with a Borate (boric acid) solution. UltraTouch meets the highest standards for fire, fungi, and corrosion resistance.

UltraTouch contains no chemical irritants or formaldehyde and requires no warning labels. Unlike fiberglass insulation, UltraTouch does not itch, is easy to handle, and can be installed without the use of protective clothing.

UltraTouch offers an extremely high noise reduction coefficient (NRC) to effectively reduce airborne sound transmissions, resulting in exceptional soundproofing in every room.

REPURPOSED MATERIAL

CONTENTS
Recycled cotton/denim fibers (85% post-industrial content)

APPLICATIONS
Interior and exterior wall, ceiling, and floor insulation

TYPES / SIZES
R-13/16" (2.1 cm), R-19/16" (3 cm), R-13/24" (1.4 cm), R-19/24" (2 cm)

ENVIRONMENTAL
Recycled content, no VOCs or harmful chemicals

TESTS / EXAMINATIONS
ICC ES Evaluation Report ESR-1134

LIMITATIONS
No blow-in installation

CONTACT
Bonded Logic, Inc.
411 East Ray Road
Chandler, AZ 85225
Tel: 480-814-9114
www.bondedlogic.com
sales@bondedlogic.com

09: **LIGHT**

ELUMIN8

ELECTROLUMINESCENT LAMPS

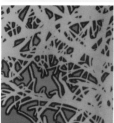

Elumin8 technology consists of applying electricity to copper dipped in zinc sulfate ink, which then emits light. This is applied using a silkscreen process to an indium tin oxide–splattered substrate. In essence, a LEC, or light emitting capacitor, is created.

The light emitted is cold, since the medium it is applied to is typically thin, such as a polyester substrate. This substrate is flexible and can be fabricated into complex shapes. The light is emitted in a uniform fashion across a given surface up to an area of approximately 3.5m^2. No ultra violet rays are emitted.

Electroluminescent lights are driven by an alternating electric field. When alternating current is applied to the ink, the electrons within the phosphor ink are excited by the intense electric field and become highly energized. This phenomenon is known as excitation. Light is emitted once the excited electrons return to a stable state. As excitation takes place whenever the direction of the electron field changes, light is emitted twice per cycle when alternating current is applied.

Standard EL lamps diminish in intensity over time and have a half-life (to fifty percent of luminosity) of approximately 3,500 hours of continuous use. The higher the current, the earlier that half-life is reached. A four hundred hertz input is more than sufficient for most uses. Elumin8 has developed new phosphors and drivers that can significantly increase the half-life of lamps.

CONTENTS

Chemically inert composition of phosphor, ceramics, and aluminum in a noncombustible envelope, printed on ITO-sputtered polyester.

APPLICATIONS

Interior design, architecture, product design, advertising point of sale

TYPES / SIZES

Custom

ENVIRONMENTAL

Energy efficient, Lambertan light source—no light pollution

CONTACT

Elumin8 Systems Ltd.
1 Nimrod Way, Ferndown
Industrial Estate, Ferndown
Dorset, BH21 7SH UK
Tel: +00 44 1202 865 100
www.elumin8.com
info@elumin8.com

EXIT

CUSTOM EMERGENCY LIGHT FIXTURE

ULTRAPERFORMING PRODUCT

EXIT is a custom exit light produced for the Nasher Sculpture Center in Dallas, Texas, where forty-two fixtures are installed. Interloop A/D designed and fabricated the exit lights, working directly with engineers, fabricators, UL technicians, and the graphic design firm 2x4. In keeping with city, state, and federal safety standards, every emergency light fixture must undergo extensive testing by the Underwriter Laboratories Testing Center to meet a wide range of design criteria. These stringent technical requirements typically thwart innovation by limiting new design, requiring the exclusive use of existing UL approved components.

With EXIT the majority of electronics are detached from the lamp itself so that the acrylic letters E-X-I-T and the minimal stainless steel brackets are the only visible elements. This approach was achieved by using a low-voltage light emitting diode (LED) configuration and light-gauge wiring so that the power source could be installed remotely, up to twenty feet from the light fixture. The letters were detached and given a thickness by milling acrylic to produce a lens with a structural shape. Custom circuit boards and stainless steel backing plates were then laminated to this translucent lens to create a stable diaphragm, eliminating the need for large enclosures or heavy brackets.

CONTENTS
Milled acrylic, light emitting diode (LED) circuit boards (cnc custom milled), stainless steel brackets and mounting plate

APPLICATIONS
Emergency and safety light fixture applications

TYPES / SIZES
3 mounting brackets: surface mount, side mount, and ceiling mount; 2 safety styles: with and without chevron

ENVIRONMENTAL
LED lamp and power set-up: energy efficient, low heat emission

TESTS / EXAMINATIONS
UL Listed

CONTACT
Interloop A/D
1406 Sul Ross
Houston, TX 77006
Tel: 713-522-0739
www.interloopdesign.com/exit.htm
exit@interloopdesign.com

INTELLIWHITE

INTELLIGENT SOLID-STATE LED LIGHTING SYSTEM

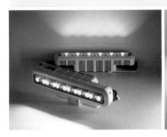

Intelliwhite is an intelligent solid-state lighting system that features variable color temperature and can produce cool to warm gradients of white light in the range of three thousand to sixty-five hundred kelvin. Intelliwhite applies Color Kinetics' Optibin technology to ensure consistent color from one fixture to the next, and its compact size and lack of radiated heat allows for versatile installation options.

Depending on the type, Intelliwhite fixtures are easily controlled by an iW Scene Controller or third-party DMX controllers. In addition to its aesthetic versatility, Intelliwhite features the inherent benefits of LED sources, including efficiency, long life, durability, and lack of UV emission.

CONTENTS
Aluminum, zinc, iron, fiberglass, silica, PVC, santoprene, nylon, PC

APPLICATIONS
Depends on type: interior/ exterior wall washing and grazing, large alcove light-ing, architectural high-lights, studio lighting, and other applications requiring variable color temperature

TYPES / SIZES
iW Blast, iW Cast, iW MR, iW Profile

ENVIRONMENTAL
LED sources consume less power and last far longer than conventional light sources, reducing waste and dependency on electric power plants. LEDs are also mercury-free and do not radiate heat or UV light

LIMITATIONS
Depends on type: not submersible and/or not for exterior use

CONTACT
Color Kinetics
10 Milk Street, Suite 1100
Boston, MA 02108
Toll-free: 888-FULL-RGB
www.colorkinetics.com
info@colorkinetics.com

INTERACTIVE FUZZY LIGHT WALL

N° 260936-002

INTERACTIVE TEXTILE SENSOR WALL PANEL

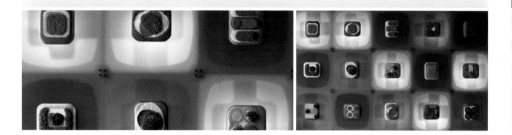

International Fashion Machines (IFM) provides private research and consulting in electronic textiles to a variety of clients, industries, and the military. They work with the latest electronic yarns and a variety of textile processes including embroidery, sewing, weaving and braiding. IFM also creates electronic textile connections, both intra-textile and between traditional electronics and textiles.

Designed by Maggie Orth and Sam Bittman, IFM's Fuzzy Light Wall consists of a matrix of capacitive sensors that dim lights on and off, illuminating colorful shapes with the soft touch of the hand. The installation hangs on a wall like any other piece of art, but unlike conventional artwork it changes color and pattern based on user interaction. IFM's products consist of hand-woven and printed computer displays, integrated with proprietary drive electronics and custom software.

TRANSFORMATIONAL PRODUCT

CONTENTS

Conductive yarns, traditional light fixtures, plexiglass, incandescent light bulbs, theater gels, wood

APPLICATIONS

Lighting, interactive art, theater

TYPES / SIZES

5 × 3' (1.5 × .9 m)

CONTACT

International Fashion Machines
1205 East Pike Street
Suite 2G
Seattle, WA 98112
Tel: 206-860-5166
www.ifmachines.com
info@ifmachines.com

LIGHTFADER

INTERACTIVE LIGHT FLOOR

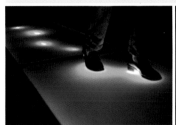
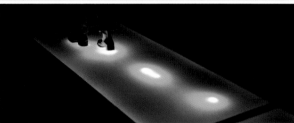

When a pedestrian walks across Rogier Sterk's interactive light floor, his or her weight displaces fluid contained within the panel system, leaving "light prints" for about one minute after contact. The system may be constructed as an independent floor and can perform without the built-in light. In this configuration, footprints allow light within an upper space to be visible from below.

CONTENTS
Plastic, T1 lights

APPLICATIONS
Flooring in interior and exterior public facilities, from bars, restaurants, and waiting rooms to cinemas and entrances to office buildings; direction indicators in department stores and airports

TYPES / SIZES
39.5 × 39.5" (100 × 100 cm); other dimensions on request

ENVIRONMENTAL
Low energy, useful lamp life 50,000 hours

TESTS / EXAMINATIONS
IP 54, CE

CONTACT
TAL
Joos De Ter Beerstlaan 33
Pittem, 8740 Belgium
Tel: +0031 26 4451600
www.tal.be
info@tal.be

LIGHT DIFFUSION AND CONTROL TECHNOLOGY

MesoOptics technology offers an innovative way to purify and control light with exceptional energy efficiency. MesoOptics material is produced using proprietary patterns of microstructures that are created using holographic techniques and replicated on a suitable substrate such as acrylic, poly-carbonate, or glass. These microstructures give MesoOptics material advanced optical capabilities that minimize shadows and glare and create uniquely luminous environments with enhanced visual comfort.

MesoOptics removes striations and hot spots from lighting sources, creating smooth gradients of pure, white light, free from color shifts. MesoOptics can constrain or disperse lighting for optimum control and uniformity: a wide beam of light can be constrained into a small area, or a small beam of light can be dispersed into a wider area. The microstructures can be configured to produce a range of beam shapes from linear through elliptical and circular. MesoOptics technology can also redirect light to desired angles regardless of the angle of input.

MesoOptics is a highly transmissive material that allows up to ninety-five percent of the light that enters to pass through. This enables the development of energy-efficient products that are environmentally responsible and visually healthy.

CONTENTS
100% acrylic

APPLICATIONS
Light diffusion and control, skylight and window films, backlighting LCD screens

ENVIRONMENTAL
Enhances energy efficiency

LIMITATIONS
Not suggested for applications with high heat or abrasive environments

CONTACT
Ledalite Architectural Products
19750 92A Avenue
Langley, BC V1M 3B2
Canada
Tel: 604-888-6811
www.ledalite.com
mesooptics@ledalite.com

INTELLIGENT MATERIAL

SUNLIGHT TRANSPORTING SYSTEM

INTELLIGENT PRODUCT

Parans Daylight AB has developed a sunlight transmission system for buildings that consists of three parts: the light-collecting panel, SkyPort; the light-transporting cable, SunWire; and the light-emitting luminaries, Björk.

The patent pending SkyPort is Parans's primary innovation. Two layers of optics are mounted inside the panels, each consisting of 576 lenses made from the polymer PMMA. The upper layer tracks the sun, adjusted by a sun-tracking sensor, electronics, and stepping motors. Each installation is specified according to the amount of light required and how far it should be transported. The SkyPort panels are easily mounted to any roof structure.

The flexible SunWire cable transports the sunlight captured by the SkyPort panels via bundled fiber optic cables. SunWire is designed for easy installation, even in existing buildings.

The Björk luminaires emit the transported sunlight as a mixture of parallel light beams and ambient light, just as when the sun strikes through the foliage of a forest (hence the name Björk, which is Swedish for birch tree).

The Parans system allows building occupants to monitor the weather even in the absence of windows or skylights, thus re-establishing a connection with the outside environment. Natural light has been proven to help regulate human body functions, such as body temperature, awareness, and immune system activity.

CONTENTS
SkyPort: Stainless steel, PMMA; Björk: Acrylic, PMMA; SunWire: fiber optic cables

APPLICATIONS
Daylighting

TYPES / SIZES
SkyPort outdoor sunpanel: 23.5 × 23.5 × 4" (60 × 60 × 10 cm);

Björk indoor luminaire: large 23.5 × 23.5 × 3" (60 × 60 × 7 cm), small 12 × 12 × 3" (30 × 30 × 7 cm); SunWire sunlight-transporting fiber optic cable

ENVIRONMENTAL
Reduced energy consumption as a result of less artificial lighting and less HVAC use

LIMITATIONS
Maximum cable length 15m, SkyPort requires exposure to sunlight

CONTACT
Parans Daylight AB
Eklandagatan 4
Göteborg, 412 55 Sweden
Tel: +0046 31 20 15 90
www.parans.com

SPLIT BLOCK

SCULPTURAL UNFOLDING LIGHT

The Split Block represents the exploration of transformation and reconfigurability with a light sculpture. At first glance, it appears to be a simple cuboid form with a stainless steel exterior. When opened along the split, however, the steel block reveals illuminated planes and a glowing interior. The Split Block may be reconfigured in different positions and can even be turned inside out, transforming itself into a fractured luminous prism.

CONTENTS
Stainless steel, acrylic, 12 V light sources

APPLICATIONS
Light, sculpture

TYPES / SIZES
Compacted: 22 × 22 × 23.5" (56 × 56 × 60 cm); extended: 71 × 23.5 × 27.5" (180 × 60 × 70 cm)

LIMITATIONS
Not for exterior use

CONTACT
Korban Flaubert
8/8-10 Burrows Road
St. Peters, NSW 2044
Australia
Tel: +61-2-95576136
www.korbanflaubert.
com.au

SPORE

LED ILLUMINATED PUSH BUTTON

Tom Gordon and Ted Pierson designed the spOre buttons for their own homes, intending to make a positive first impression on visitors. spOre doorbell buttons are unusual in their use of energy-efficient LEDs as a light source. The transparent resin button provides soft tactile feedback, and the button housing is finished with machined anodized aluminum hardware.

CONTENTS
60% thermoplastic elastomeric resin, 35% aluminum, 5% stainless steel

APPLICATIONS
Doorbell, call button, interactive displays, electric garage doors, home automation systems, low voltage decorative lighting

TYPES / SIZES
Square 2.8 × 2.8" (7.2 × 7.2 cm), round 2.7" (6.9 cm) diameter

ENVIRONMENTAL
Energy efficient, low heat output

CONTACT
spOre
PO Box 4758
Seattle, WA 98194
Tel: 206-624-9573
www.sporeinc.com
info@sporeinc.com

TEMPORAL LIGHT

ELECTROLUMINESCENT WALL TILES

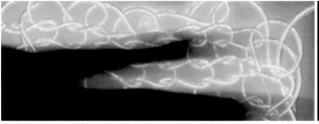

Rachel Wingfield's Temporal Light is a tiling system designed to illuminate public and private spaces. The system utilizes knitted electroluminescent wire cast in resin with electronics. Each tile forms a pixel that responds to a moving shadow being cast upon it, mapping a physical pathway with an inverted, illuminating shadow. Light trails linger as one moves through space, providing localized and personal illumination.

CONTENTS
Resin, electroluminescent wire, electronics

APPLICATIONS
Light, wall tile

TYPES / SIZES
6 × 6" (15 × 15 cm) standard size, custom sizes available

LIMITATIONS
Not for exterior use

CONTACT
Loop.pH
11 Springfield House,
5 Tyssen Street
London, E8 2LY UK
Tel: +44 (0)7792474091
www.loop.ph
loop@loop.ph

THERAPIE

ILLUMINATED CANVAS

Inspired by color and light therapy studies, Andre Keilani designed Therapie to be a singular illumi-nated canvas that imparts a soothing aura. The color photons emanating from the lamp are intended to reduce stress and create a peaceful mood. Each Therapie lamp also includes an assortment of three color acetates for customizable mood generation.

CONTENTS
Aluminum frame, white lacquered steel fixture, stretched PVC canvas, fluo-rescent tube

APPLICATIONS
Wall lamp

TYPES / SIZES
Therapie 1842:
7 × 16.5 × 1.5"
(18 × 42 × 3.75 cm);
1953: 7.5 × 21 × 1.5"
(19 × 53 × 3.75 cm);
2066: 8 × 26 × 1.5"
(20 × 66 × 3.75 cm);
2626: 10 × 10 × 1.5"
(26 × 26 × 3.75 cm)

ENVIRONMENTAL
Enhances indoor environ-mental quality via visual stress reduction

LIMITATIONS
Not for exterior use

CONTACT
Snowlab Design, Inc.
24 Avenue du Mont-Royal
Quest, Suite 503B
Montreal, Quebec H2T 252
Canada
Tel: 212-925-5506
www.snowlabdesign.com
info@modobjects.net

TILED WALL

INTERACTIVE CERAMIC LIGHT WALL

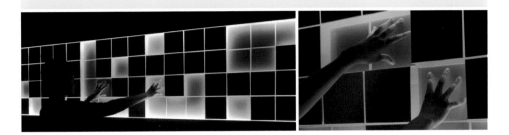

Made of ceramic tiles projecting from an illuminated background, Rogier Sterk's Tiled Wall offers users an opportunity to play with light. Each tile is attached to a mechanism that allows it to be pressed and released. A tile left untouched appears to be lit only around the edges. Once a tile is pressed, however, the underlying light shines across its surface, emitting a reflection. The amount of light emitted is therefore determined by the position of the tiles.

CONTENTS
Ceramic tiles, fluorescent lighting, framework

APPLICATIONS
Lighting, feature wall, interactive sculpture

ENVIRONMENTAL
Low-energy light source

CONTACT
TAL
Joos De Ter Beerstlaan 33
Pittem, 8740 Belgium
Tel: +0031 26 4451600
www.tal.be
info@tal.be

TRANSFORMATIONAL PRODUCT

10: **DIGITAL**

BODY BRUSH

INTERACTIVE DIGITAL BODY PAINTING

 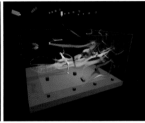 

Body Brush is a real-time body-driven immersive experience. It captures spatial human motion data and transforms it into a rich variety of 3D visual forms that are visualized through a stereo projector and has 3D sound.

The Body Brush process is achieved with the development of a low-cost computer-vision–based motion analysis system using frontal infrared illumination in addition to an innovative graphic rendering software, which translates anatomical gestures into 3D digital pathways.

Professional visual artists can use this intuitive interface to create rich 2D, 3D, or animated visual artwork. Since the tracking system can be easily adapted to stage lighting, stage setup, and costumes, the Body Brush interface can augment live performances with real-time interaction between dancers or actors, the audiovisual output, and the machine. Research is also currently being conducted to transform the Body Brush interface into a semi-immersive virtual environment with body-driven audiovisual feedback for therapeutic applications.

CONTENTS
SGI Octane 2, Octane 1,
IR Lights, Sony CCTV
Cameras, Barco Projector
SIM 6, Apple MAC G4,
Sound Module, 5.1 Speaker,
Black Drape

APPLICATIONS
Digital painting and sculpting, augmented theatrical
stage, therapy, education

TYPES / SIZES
Screen size: 29.5 × 29.5 ×
39.4' (9 × 9 × 12 m)

LIMITATIONS
Not for exterior use

CONTACT
IMVR Lab, City University
of Hong Kong
83 Tat Chee Avenue
Kowloon
Hong Kong, China
Tel: +852 2788 8580
www.cs.cityu.edu.
hk/~bodybrush

A PROCESS THAT CREATES 3D IMAGERY OF THE GROUND SUBSURFACE

 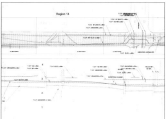 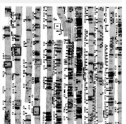

INTERFACIAL PROCESS

The lack of accurate infrastructure mapping has resulted in the loss of billions of dollars annually, in addition to needless physical harm. Infrastructure documentation is notoriously inadequate, and accidents often occur when workers cut lines without being aware of their existence (gas, sewer, steam, electricity, etc.). Designed by Alan Witten, Computer Assisted Radar Tomography (CART) is intended to solve these problems by making the invisible visible.

CART is a patented combination of hardware and software that creates spatially accurate, high-resolution 3D imagery of the shallow subsurface from zero to ten feet below grade. Computer video files are created using a rapid-fire ground-penetrating radar antenna, a survey-grade robotic laser tracking system, and patented image-processing software. In these files, utility infrastructure and other subsurface features can be seen and may be extracted and rendered in CAD or GIS.

CONTENTS
Hardware, software

APPLICATIONS
Subsurface characterization: subsurface utility engineering, utility design and construction, environmental site assessment, forensic investigation, roadbed/bridgedeck assessment, UXO detection

ENVIRONMENTAL
Reduces risk, cost, damage, service interruptions, loss of life, etc. normally associated with lack of adequate and/or accurate subsurface characterization

TESTS / EXAMINATIONS
American Society of Civil Engineers Standard 38-02

LIMITATIONS
Not applicable in areas with highly-conductive soils (e.g. Great Salt Lake area) or limited depth of penetration

CONTACT
Witten Technologies, Inc.
1365 Windsor Harbor Drive
Jacksonville, FL 32225
Tel: 813-839-5457
www.wittentech.com

E INK

ELECTRONIC INK

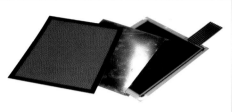

Electronic ink consists of an electronically coated optical film used in the manufacturing of high contrast, sunlight-readable, ultra-low–power electronic paper displays. The principal components of electronic ink are millions of tiny microcapsules, which are about the diameter of a human hair. In one incarnation, each microcapsule contains positively charged white particles and negatively charged black particles suspended in a clear fluid. When a negative electric field is applied, the white particles move to the top of the microcapsule where they become visible to the user. This makes the surface appear white at that spot.

To form an E Ink electronic display, the ink is printed onto a sheet of plastic film that is laminated to a layer of circuitry. The circuitry forms a pattern of pixels that can then be controlled by a display driver. These microcapsules are suspended in a liquid carrier medium, allowing them to be printed using existing screen printing processes onto virtually any surface, including glass, plastic, fabric, and even paper. Ultimately, electronic ink will permit most any surface to become a display, bringing information out of the confines of traditional devices and into the world around us.

CONTENTS
Plastic film, electronic
ink coating

APPLICATIONS
Public information displays,
handheld electronic reading
devices, advertising and
promotion displays, electronic shelf labels, watches,
clocks, smartcards, medical
devices, consumer electronics, industrial indicators,
mobile phones

TYPES / SIZES
14 × 9.5" (36 × 24 cm) maximum display size

ENVIRONMENTAL
Ultra-low power required

CONTACT
E Ink Corporation
733 Concord Avenue
Cambridge, MA 02138
Tel: 617-499-6000
www.eink.com
sales@eink.com

VIRTUAL LUMINAIRE MODELS FOR DIGITAL LIGHTING SIMULATION

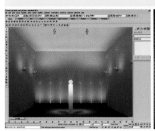  

INTERFACIAL PROCESS

ERCO virtual luminaires are digital fixtures that accurately predict how their real counterparts will behave. Architecture begins in the mind. The progress from concept to reality takes time and can require considerable persuasion. In this regard, implementing architectural design is largely a matter of communication. As spatial perception is entirely visual, computer-generated visualizations have rapidly gained a permanent place in the process of architectural design. Just as in real architecture, virtual architecture only comes to life with light.

Therefore, every ERCO luminaire has a virtual "twin" in the form of digital luminaire data, which can be downloaded from the web site and inserted directly into lighting simulation and visualization software to enable physically accurate studies, visualizations, and analyses with photographic-quality.

CONTENTS
Data

APPLICATIONS
Lighting simulation studies, architectural visualizations, animations, or computer game scenes

TYPES / SIZES
VIZ files for use in AUTODESK VIZ software containing 3D Volume Data including Joints for Inverse Kinematics, Surface/Color Data, Photometric Data (IES format)

ENVIRONMENTAL
Lighting simulation studies may protect the environment from the negative effects of bad lighting solutions, such as waste of energy, light pollution, or glare

CONTACT
ERCO Leuchten GmbH
Brockhauser Weg 80-82
Lüdenscheid, 58507
Germany
Tel: +49 2351 551 100
www.erco.com
info@erco.com

INTERACTABLE

INTERACTIVE TABLE

Andreas Störiko designed the InteracTable in order to answer questions regarding the nature of work in the new millennium: Why does an increasing rate of media discontinuity block our thinking although it is the digital age? What should furniture that allows teamwork on the computer look like? What would a digital work environment that actually encourages creativity look like?

The InteracTable is a high table with a large-format, interactive screen integrated into the top surface, which serves as a shared working platform for project groups. The InteracTable combines high technology with familiar work practices; it is operated by a pen or a finger instead of a keyboard or mouse.

The design as a "normal" high table creates a familiar atmosphere for discussions and allows natural integration within seminar and conference spaces. Most importantly, the InteracTable provides a meeting place in an infomal atmosphere for all those involved in a project. Such a work environment promotes creativity and innovation and supports shared processing of complex information structures such as project plans and engineering drawings.

CONTENTS
Steel, wood, computer hardware, display, interactive overlay

APPLICATIONS
Conference rooms, training and seminar rooms, showrooms, exhibitions, project rooms

TYPES / SIZES
Table: 87 × 47/39 × 37"
(220 × 120/99 × 95 cm);
effective display size:
43 × 24" (110 × 62 cm)

CONTACT
Foresee
Hauptstrasse 81
Bad Münder, 31848
Germany
Tel: +49 172 5449988
www.foresee.biz

DIGITALLY CONTROLLED RESPONSIVE SHOP WINDOW

Designed by Sensing Places's Flavia Sparacino, the Interactive Shop Window is an installation driven by the movement of people walking in the street. The setup includes a large and bright LCD (or LED) display placed inside the shop window facing outside towards the street. A wide-angle video camera connected to computer-running custom-vision software is used to track the passage of people in the street. The system detects pedestrian presence, speed, and distance from the window.

The interactive content of the shop window is designed according to the specific needs of the shop, the merchandise on sale, or the communication strategy of the vendor. Sensing Places's most recent installation features responsive portraits, which are short video loops of people portrayed in various expressions. The portraits are responsive to passersby: the way in which pedestrians walk in front of the window causes a change in mood of the portrait, determining a switch of expression from neutral to happy, or from boredom to surprise, scorn, love, anger, etc.

CONTENTS
Computer-vision people-tracking software, multimedia orchestration software, computers, cameras, display

APPLICATIONS
Advertising, corporate communication, public art

TYPES / SIZES
Can scale from a regular shop window size to the entire surface of a building facade

LIMITATIONS
No force-feedback available with camera-based input devices

CONTACT
Sensing Places
One Broadway, Suite 600
Cambridge, MA 02142
Tel: 617-899-7001
www.sensingplaces.com
info@sensingplaces.com

INTERFACIAL PRODUCT

INTERWALL

INTERACTIVE HOLOGRAPHIC WALL

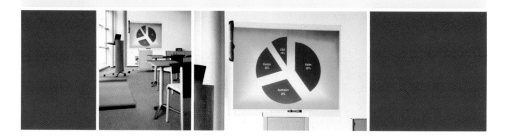

Teams need team computers: until now, working with a personal computer has only been possible for individuals. With the InterWall, it is possible to use a digital environment for teamwork, presentations, and conferences. Presentations and graphics in any required file format are projected onto the InterWall, which is a holographic glass surface. In this way, the product only becomes a display surface when it is in use; otherwise it is completely transparent. The mobile frame also allows flexible and fast application in different situations: as an electronic white board, a flip chart, a pin board, or a presentation and interaction surface for trade fairs and reception areas.

The InterWall is designed to increase work effectiveness within a given space. It allows the elimination of media and process discontinuity between individual work and teamwork, as well as the networking of work groups at different locations, which can lead to considerable time and cost savings.

CONTENTS
Steel, safety glass with
holographic film

TYPES / SIZES
52 × 31.5 × 77"
(132 × 80 × 195 cm)

APPLICATIONS
Conference rooms, training
and seminar rooms, show-
rooms, fairs

CONTACT
Foresee
Hauptstrasse 81
Bad Münder, 31848
Germany
Tel: +49 172 5449988
www.foresee.biz

LAMINA 1.0

SOFTWARE THAT FACILITATES CONSTRUCTION OF PRECISE FREE-FORM STRUCTURES FROM SHEET MATERIAL

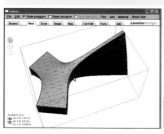  

Designed by Paul Haeberli, Lamina 1.0 software facilitates the fabrication of large-scale free-form structures from planar materials like plastic, metal, or plywood. This fabrication technology can be applied to interior design, architecture, lighting, signage, and sculpture.

Lamina 1.0 uses a computer process to build precise physical structures. A user's 3D model is approximated by a number of 2D parts that are numerically cut and attached to fabricate the final structure. Laser-cutting, abrasive waterjet-cutting and plasma-cutting services are widely available and make creating parts inexpensive and fast.

This software accounts for the physical behavior of planar materials and uses the material thickness to inset the edges of cutting paths to make parts that fit together with precision. Where parts join at right angles, the inset for an edge to edge joint is half the material thickness. The angle between parts is also taken into consideration when generating cutting path insets; thus, the join angle and the appropriate inset may vary along edges. A demo version of the program can be downloaded from the web site.

CONTENTS

Software

APPLICATIONS

Sculpture fabrication, interior design, building architecture, lighting, and furniture

TYPES / SIZES

Accepts OBJ and 3DS formats; Lamina creates 2D cutting paths in DXF format.

ENVIRONMENTAL

Allows for highly efficient use of material

CONTACT

Lamina Design
2560 Kendall Avenue
Madison, WI 53705
Tel: 608-772-3616
www.laminadesign.com
info@laminadesign.com

TEXXUS

DIGITALLY CONTROLLED SURFACE MANIPULATION OF MATERIALS

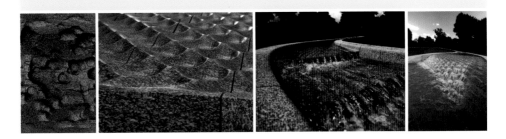

Texxus creates 3D surface forms and textures for architectural, industrial, and consumer products. Using advanced modeling and production software, Texxus creates surfaces at any scale and produces them in suitable materials using computer-controlled manufacturing technology. Previously unachievable organic free-form shapes of almost any size can now be produced to engineering tolerances by one of the most advanced CAD/CAM design and manufacturing facilities in Europe.

The Texxus process regards both the 3D surface geometry as well as an optional superimposed 3D texture relief and interfaces with a number of output manufacturing technologies, which have joint ventures in stonework and pattern-making for foundry work, such as aero-aluminum, bronze, and cast iron. In this way, Texxus is able to enhance the appearance, performance, and value of surfaces.

CONTENTS
Software

APPLICATIONS
Advanced surface manipu-
lation for architecture and
industrial design

ENVIRONMENTAL
Precise control of material
quantities

CONTACT
Texxus
5 Delancey Passage,
Delancey Street
London, NW1 7NN UK
Tel: +44 (0) 20 7387 7295
www.texxus.com

INDEX

DESIGNER INDEX

MANUFACTURER INDEX

PRODUCT INDEX

ACKNOWLEDGMENTS

I would like to thank Mark Wamble for asking me to research materials for an important project at our office in 1998. If he had not pushed me, this book would probably not exist. I would also like to thank Bill Cannady and Kyle Fisher for their guidance and collaboration during this experience.

I thank my peers who have supported me, especially Andrew McCune, who greatly influenced my decision to start a catalog of innovative materials.

I give many thanks to those who supported the development of my product research effort at NBBJ, especially Lilian Asperin-Clyman, Bill Bain, Friedl Bohm, Craig Brookes, Rick Buckley, Louisa Chang, Gary Cruce, Rich Dallam, Shahana Dattagupta, Paul Davis, Helen Dimoff, Steve Doub, Bonnie Duncan, Lori Fulsaas, Cece Haw, Anita Hornby, Jim Jonassen, Alex Maxim, Patrick Mays, Steve McConnell, Joey Myers, Eric Phillips, Tim Sadler, John Savo, Bob Sheh, Rob Swartz, Alan Young, David Yuan, Christine Vandover, Dan White, David Whitfield, and Scott Wyatt. I would especially like to thank Tom Owens for his thoughtful legal counsel.

I am deeply indebted to the critical promotional roles played by Jack MacAllister with the Cameron MacAllister Group, Rita Catinella and Sara Hart of *Architectural Record*, the editors of *Archinect*, and Mason White with Cornell University.

I am very grateful to Kevin Lippert and Jennifer Thompson of Princeton Architectural Press for their wonderful support and guidance of this project.

I thank the recipients of my "product of the week" newsletter for their helpful suggestions and comments over the past five years. It gives me great pleasure to be connected to a global community of talented individuals who teach me new things every day.

Finally, I would like to express deep gratitude to my family for their love, patience, and support of this effort.

NOTES